Two-Hour Country Cross-Stitch

Two-Hour Country Cross-Stitch

Over 500 Designs

Susie Steadman

Sterling Publishing Co., Inc.   New York
A Sterling/Chapelle Book

For Chapelle Ltd.

Owner
Jo Packham

Editor
Amanda Beth McPeck

Staff
Joy Anckner, Malissa Boatwright,
Kass Burchett, Rebecca Christensen,
Amber Hansen, Shirley Heslop,
Holly Hollingsworth, Susan Jorgensen,
Susan Laws, Barbara Milburn, Pat Pearson,
Karmen Quinney, Leslie Ridenour,
Cindy Rooks, Cindy Stoeckl, Nancy Whitley,
and Lorrie Young.

Photography
Kevin Dilley for Hazen Photography

If you have any questions or comments or
would like information on specialty products
featured in this book, please contact:

Chapelle Ltd., Inc.   (801) 621-2777
P. O. Box 9252   (801) 621-2788 (fax)
Ogden, UT 84409

Library of Congress Cataloging-in-Publication Data

Steadman, Susie.
    Two-hour country cross-stitch : over 500 designs
    / Susie Steadman.
        p. cm.
    "A Sterling/Chapelle book."
    Includes index.
    ISBN 0-8069-6124-4
    1. Cross-stitch—Patterns.   2. Decoration and
    ornament, Rustic.
    I. Title.
    TL778.C76S76   1996
    746.44'3041—dc20   96-25871
                                              CIP

10 9 8 7 6 5 4 3 2

Published by Sterling Publishing Company,
    Inc., 387 Park Avenue South, New York,
    NY 10016
© 1996 by Chapelle Limited
Distributed in Canada by Sterling Publishing
    c/o Canadian Manda Group, One Atlantic
    Avenue, Suite 105, Toronto, Ontario,
    Canada M6K 3E7
Distributed in Great Britain and Europe by
    Cassell PLC, Wellington House, 125
    Strand, London WC2R 0BB, England
Distributed in Australia by Capricorn Link
    (Australia) Pty Ltd., P.O. Box 6651,
    Baulkham Hills, Business Centre, NSW
    2153, Australia
Printed and Bound in China

Sterling ISBN 0-8069-6124-4

Contents

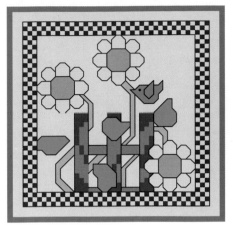

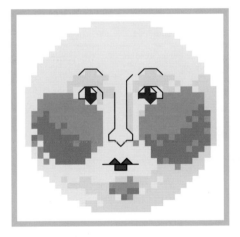

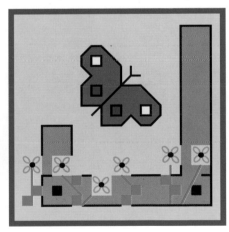

In the Garden

In the Garden

DMC Floss

	X st	BS		X st	BS
White	–		322		
3078			3755		
725			597		⌐
3825			369		
722	+		368	⊠	
721	N		320		
3328		⌐	367		
347			993		
356		⌐	991		
760			472		
3733	⊠		704	△	
407			702		
3042			3799		
932	○		336		

In the Garden

In the Garden

DMC Floss

	X st		X st	BS
White	·	3348		
743		3347		
741		3345		
740		890	N	
498	⋆	3778		
341	–	355		
340		436	+	
333		434	B	
792		801		⌐
823		938	K	

In the Garden

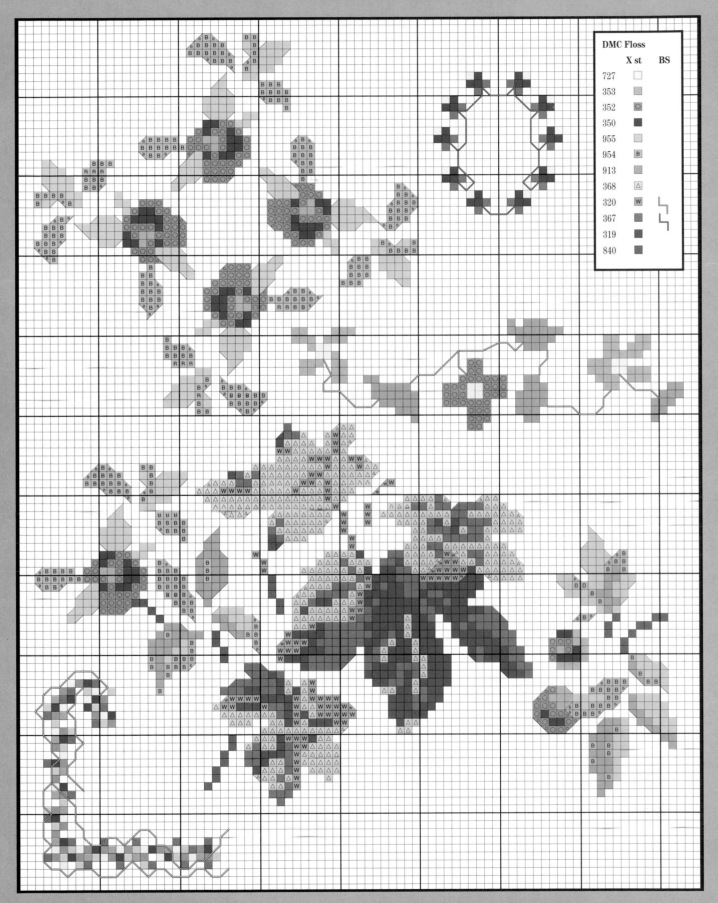

DMC Floss

	X st	BS
727	(white)	
353		
352	⊙	
350		
955		
954	B	
913		
368	△	
320	W	⌐
367		⌐
319		
840		

In the Garden

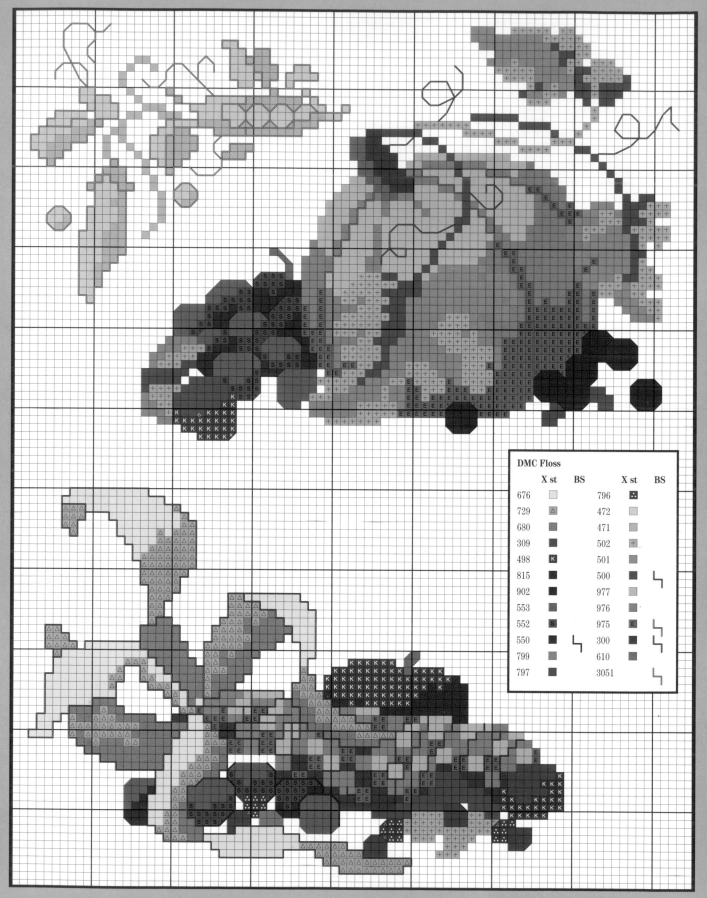

DMC Floss

	X st	BS		X st	BS
676			796		
729			472		
680			471		
309			502		
498			501		
815			500		⌐
902			977		
553			976		
552			975		⌐
550		⌐	300		⌐
799			610		
797			3051		⌐

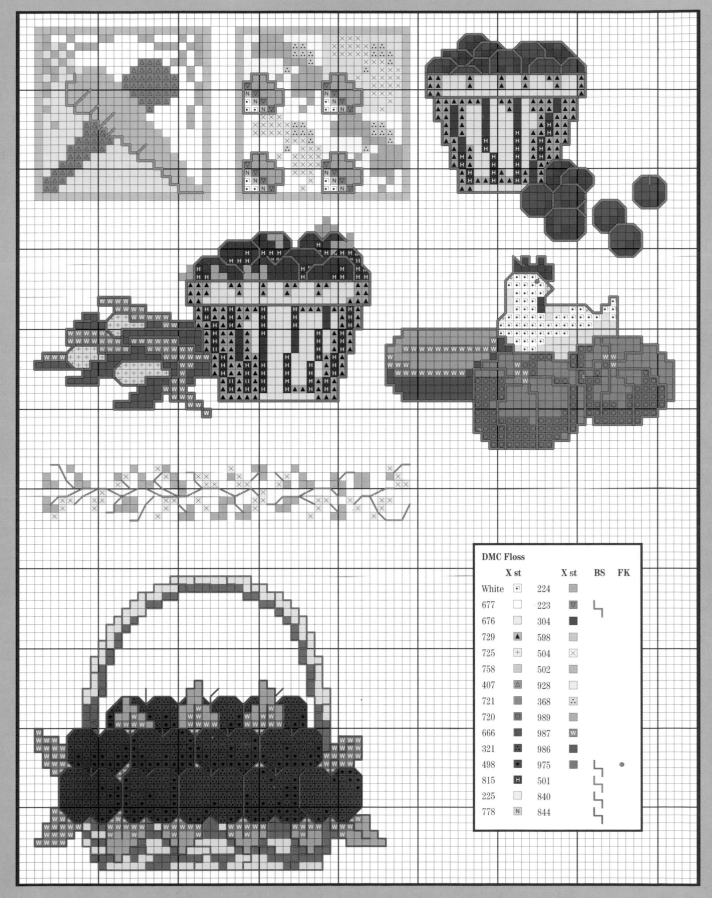

DMC Floss

	X st		X st	BS	FK
White	⊡	224			
677		223	▽	⌐	
676		304			
729	▲	598			
725	+	504	⊠		
758		502			
407	△	928			
721		368	⊡		
720	◎	989			
666		987	W		
321		986			
498	★	975		⌐	●
815	H	501		⌐	
225		840		⌐	
778	N	844		⌐	

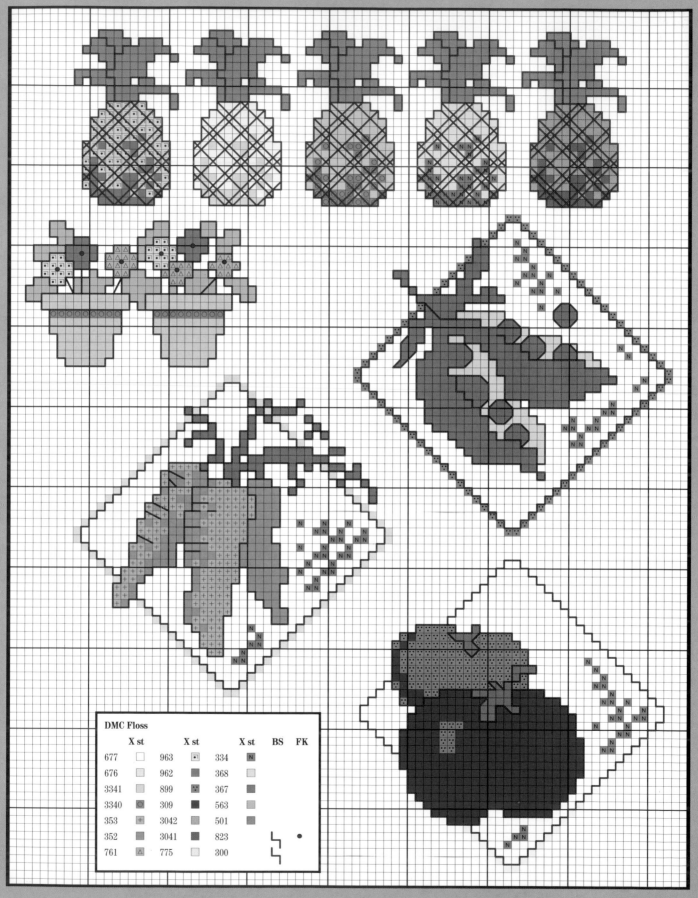

DMC Floss

	X st		X st		X st	BS	FK
677		963		334			
676		962		368			
3341		899		367			
3340		309		563			
353		3042		501			
352		3041		823			
761		775		300			●

In the Garden

DMC Floss							
	X st	X st	BS		X st	BS	
White	·	3689	⊡		597	H	
746		3688		⌐	369	⟋	
727		309			368		
951	△	304			320	⊙	⌐
758		3042			563		
3064		809			562		⌐
741		798			561		
3328		747	–		738		
225		598			729		⌐

DMC Floss

	X st	BS		X st	BS
Ecru	+		550	★	
676			796		
948	⊙		3348		
754			3347		
722			320		
3328			319		⌐
353			501		
760	✕	⌐	500		⌐
321			739		
498			435		
815			839		⌐
902			986		⌐
333			844		⌐

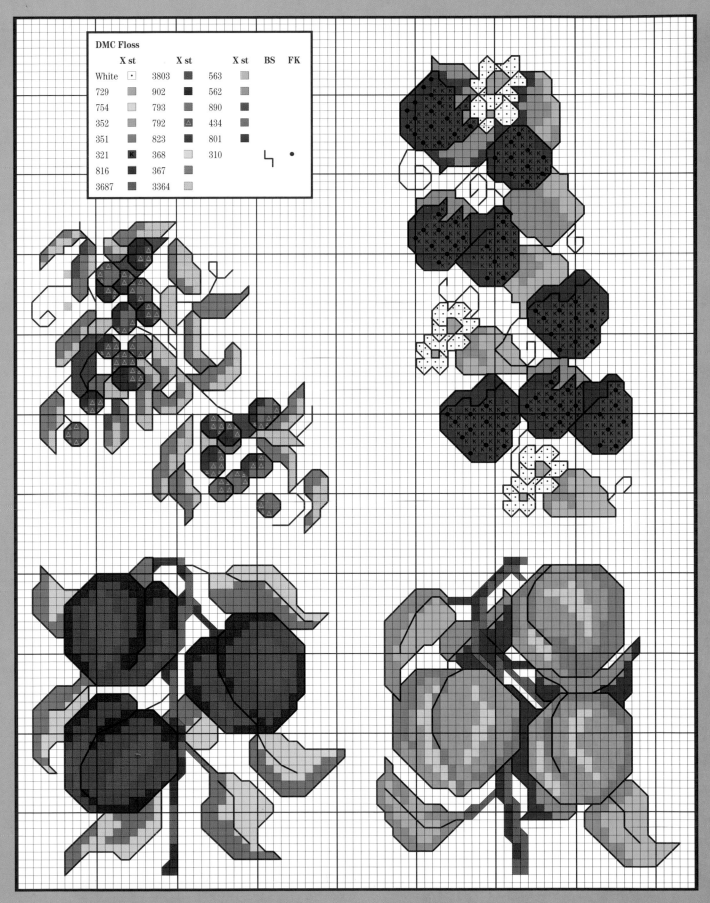

DMC Floss

	X st		X st		X st	BS	FK
White	·	3803		563			
729		902		562			
754		793		890			
352		792	△	434			
351		823		801			
321	K	368		310			
816		367					•
3687		3364					

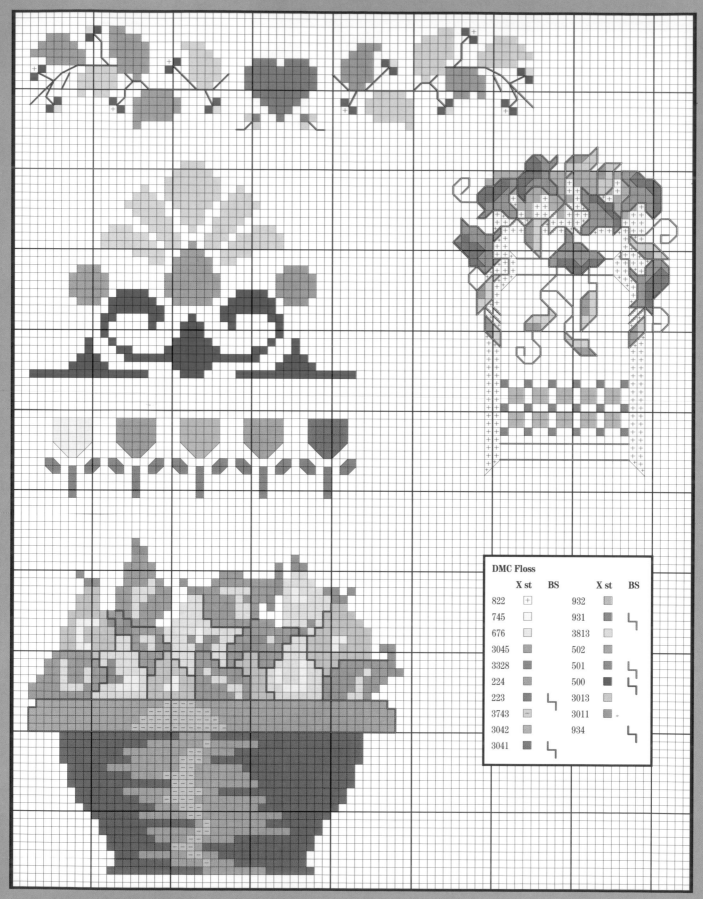

DMC Floss

	X st	BS		X st	BS
822	+		932		
745			931		⌐
676			3813		
3045			502		
3328			501		⌐
224			500		⌐
223		⌐	3013		
3743	–		3011		
3042			934		⌐
3041		⌐			

In the Garden

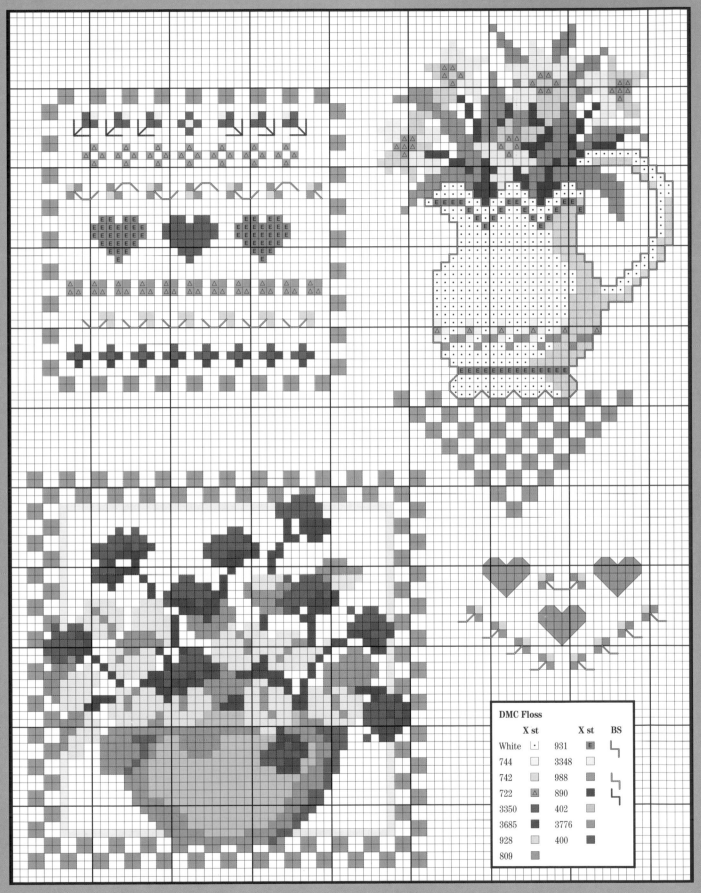

DMC Floss				
	X st		X st	BS
White	·	931	E	⌐
744		3348		
742		988		⌐
722	△	890		⌐
3350		402		
3685		3776		
928		400		
809				

In the Garden

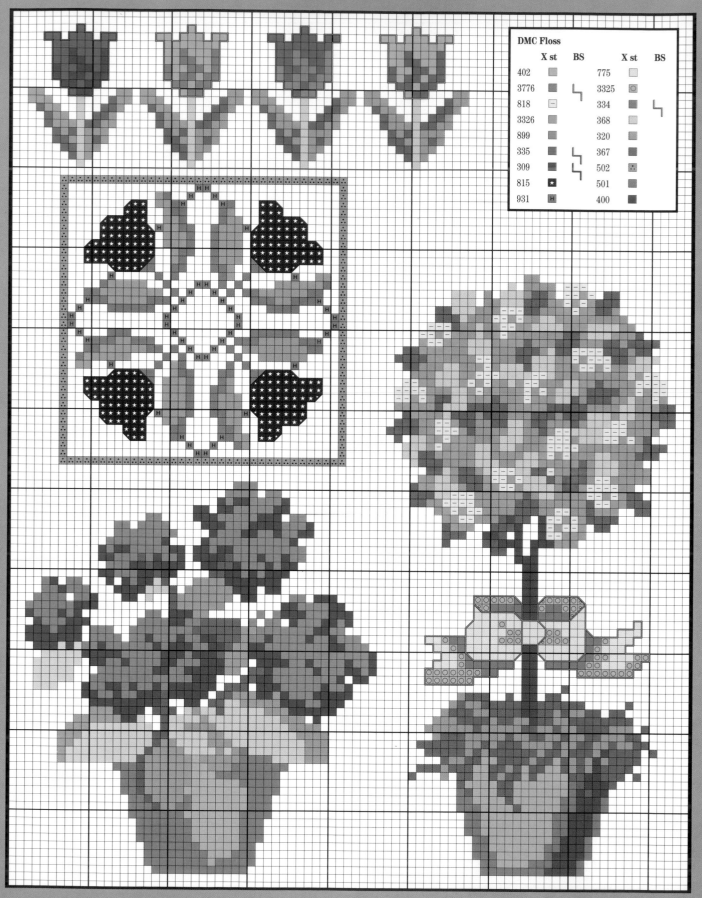

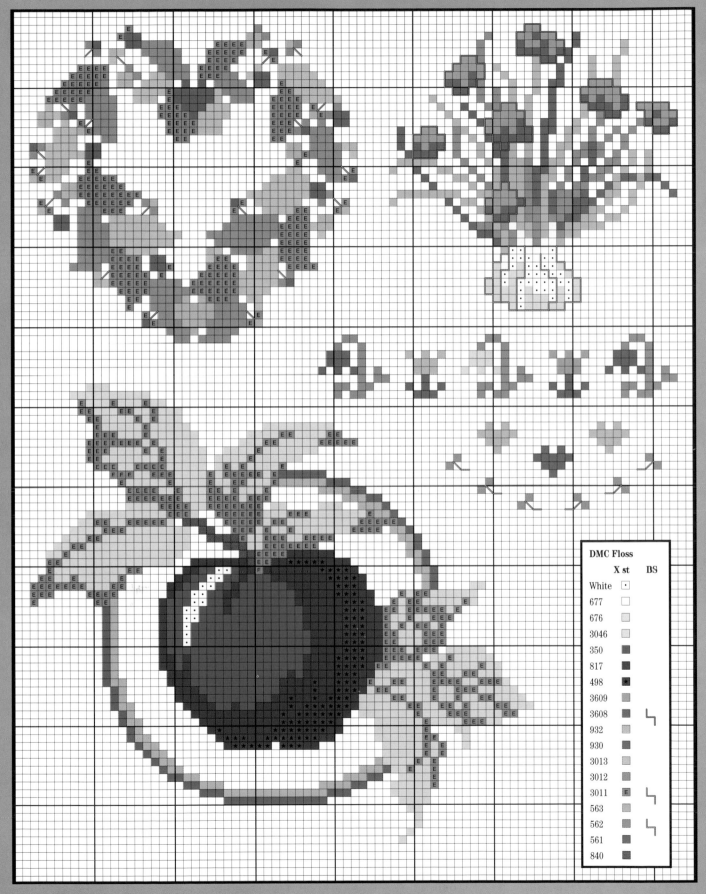

DMC Floss

	X st	BS
White	·	
677		
676		
3046		
350		
817		
498	★	
3609		
3608		⌐
932		
930		
3013		
3012		
3011	E	⌐
563		
562		⌐
561		
840		

DMC Floss	
	X st
743	
818	
605	R
604	
603	
3325	
334	
312	
368	
320	
367	

Buttons

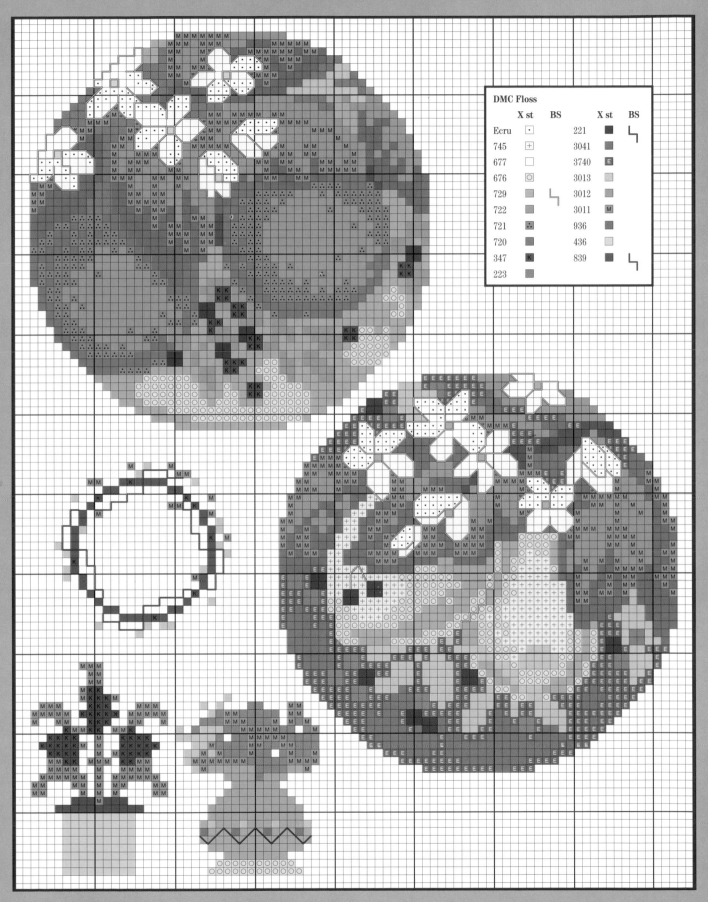

DMC Floss

	X st	BS		X st	BS
Ecru	·		221	■	⌐
745	+		3041	▩	
677	□		3740	E	
676	⊙		3013	▨	
729	▨	⌐	3012	▨	
722	▨		3011	M	
721	⊡		936	▩	
720	▨		436	▨	
347	K		839	■	⌐
223	▨				

In the Garden

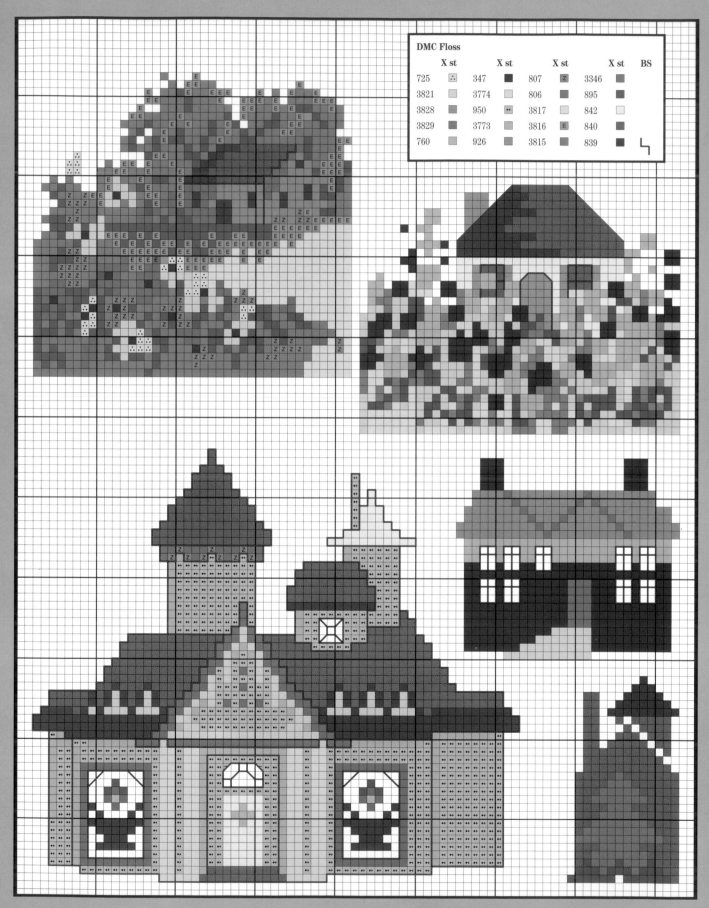

DMC Floss

X st		X st		X st		X st		BS
725	⋰	347	■	807	Z	3346	■	
3821	■	3774	■	806	■	895	■	
3828	■	950	••	3817	■	842	■	
3829	■	3773	■	3816	E	840	■	
760	■	926	■	3815	■	839	■	⌐

In the Garden

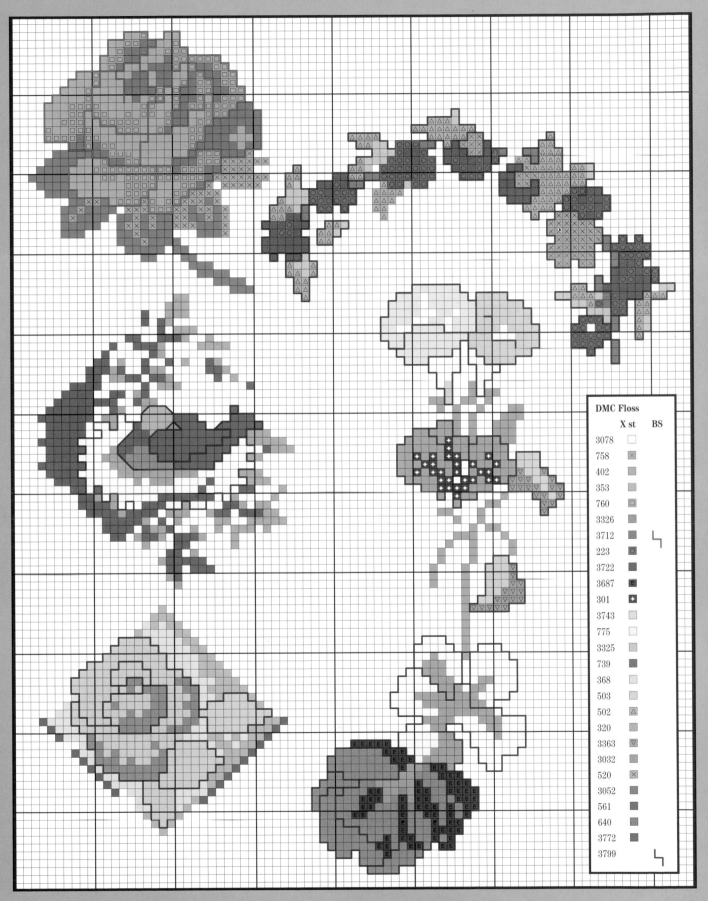

DMC Floss		
	X st	BS
3078		
758		
402		
353		
760		
3326		
3712		⌐
223		
3722		
3687	E	
301	✤	
3743		
775		
3325		
739		
368		
503		
502	△	
320		
3363	▽	
3032		
520		
3052		
561		
640		
3772		
3799		⌐

In the Garden

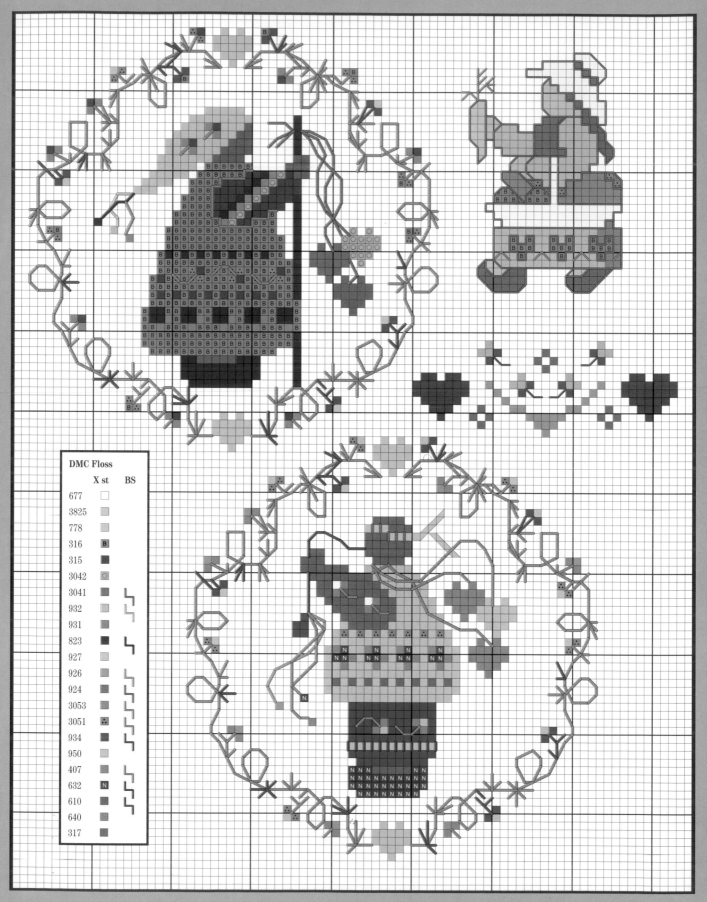

DMC Floss

	X st	BS
677		
3825		
778		
316	B	
315		
3042	⊙	
3041		
932		
931		
823		
927		
926		
924		
3053		
3051		
934		
950		
407		
632	N	
610		
640		
317		

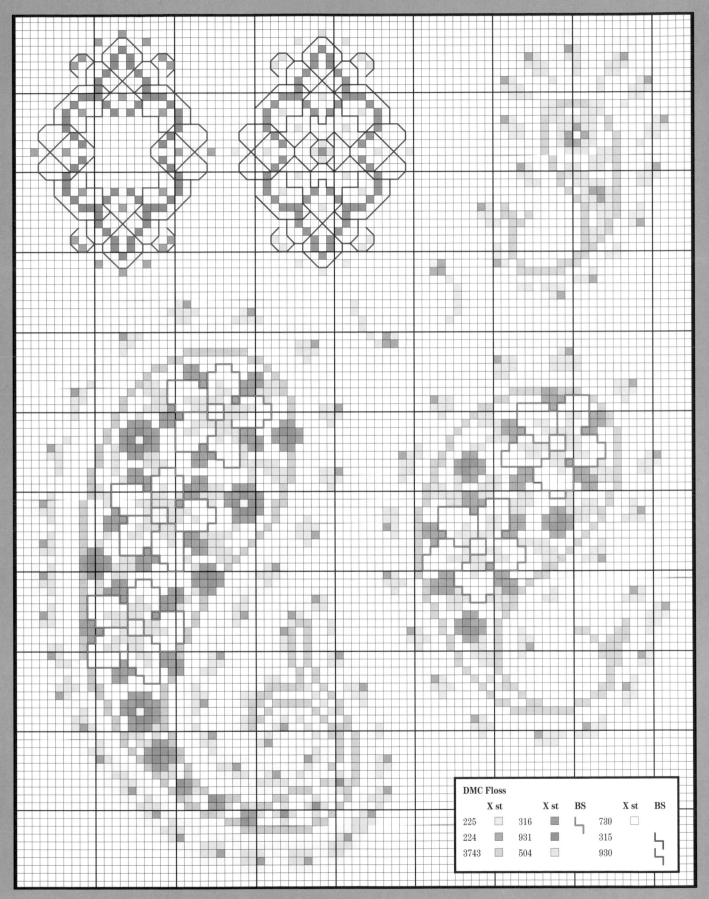

DMC Floss

	X st		X st	BS		X st	BS
225		316		⌐	730		
224		931			315		
3743		504			930		

For All Seasons

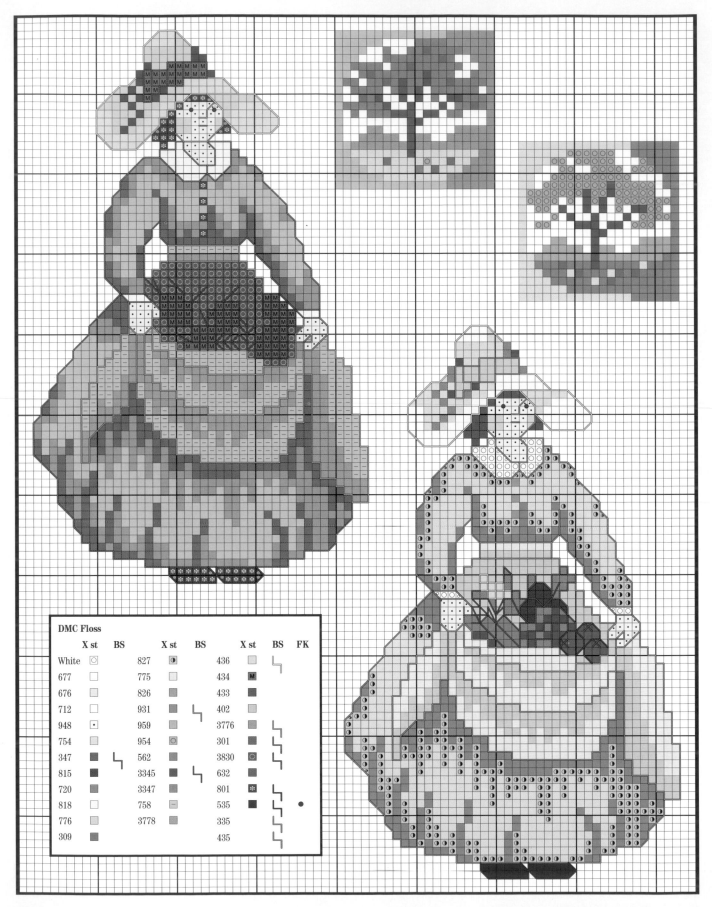

DMC Floss

	X st	BS		X st	BS		X st	BS	FK
White	⊙		827	◑		436		⌐	
677			775			434	M		
676			826			433			
712			931		⌐	402			
948	·		959			3776		⌐	
754			954	○		301		⌐	
347		⌐	562			3830	◎	⌐	
815			3345		⌐	632			
720			3347			801	❋	⌐	
818			758	–		535		⌐	●
776			3778			335		⌐	
309						435		⌐	

For All Seasons

DMC Floss

	X st	BS		X st	BS		X st	BS	FK
White			326			959			
3823			815			3817			
745			433		⌐	3816			
743			224			3815			
729		⌐	223			367			
948			3721			500			
712			3806			632		⌐	
754			554			535		⌐	●
721			3807			221		⌐	
435		⌐	772			553		⌐	

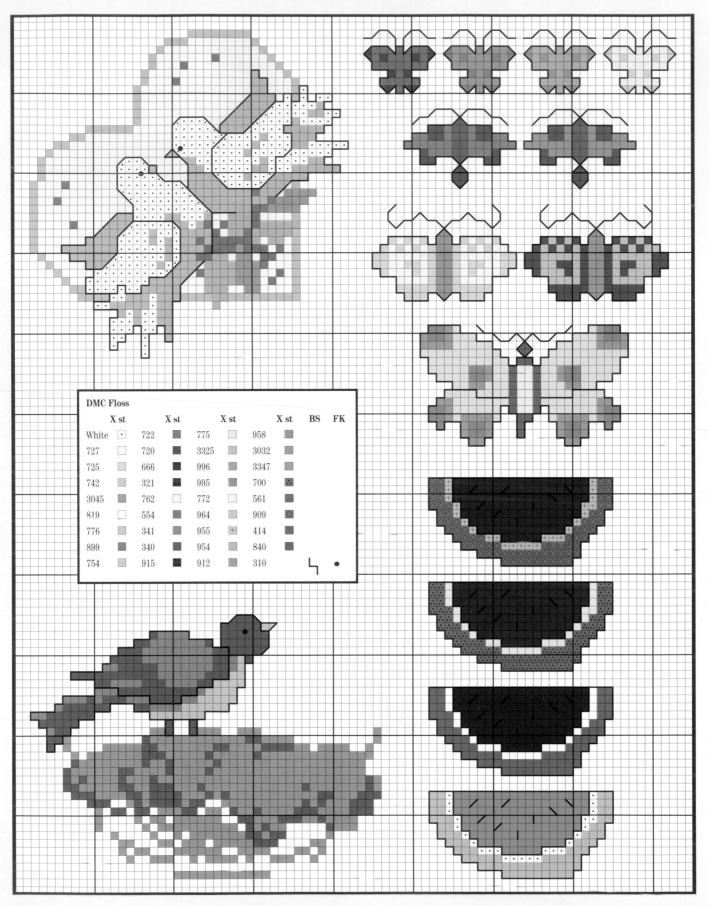

DMC Floss

	X st		X st		X st		X st	BS	FK
White	·	722	■	775		958	■		
727		720	■	3325		3032	■		
725		666	■	996		3347			
742		321	■	995		700	▨		
3045		762		772		561			
819		554		964		909	◉		
776		341		955	+	414			
899		340		954		840			
754		915	■	912		310		⌐	●

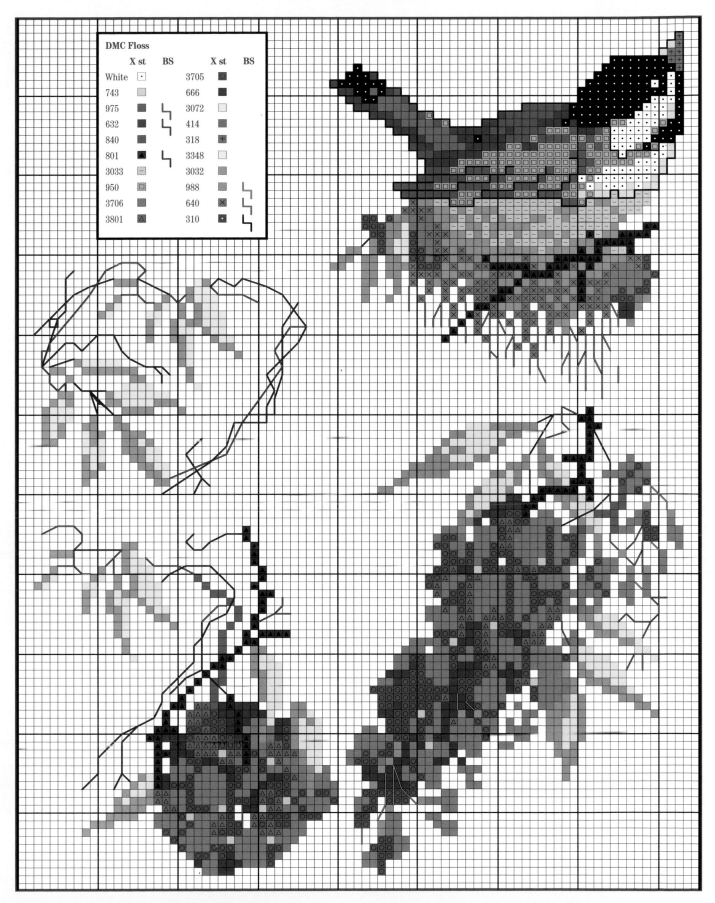

DMC Floss

	X st	BS		X st	BS
White	·		3705		
743			666		
975		⌐	3072		
632		⌐	414		
840			318	+	
801	▲	⌐	3348		
3033	–		3032		
950	▣		988		⌐
3706			640	✕	⌐
3801	△		310	▪	⌐

For All Seasons

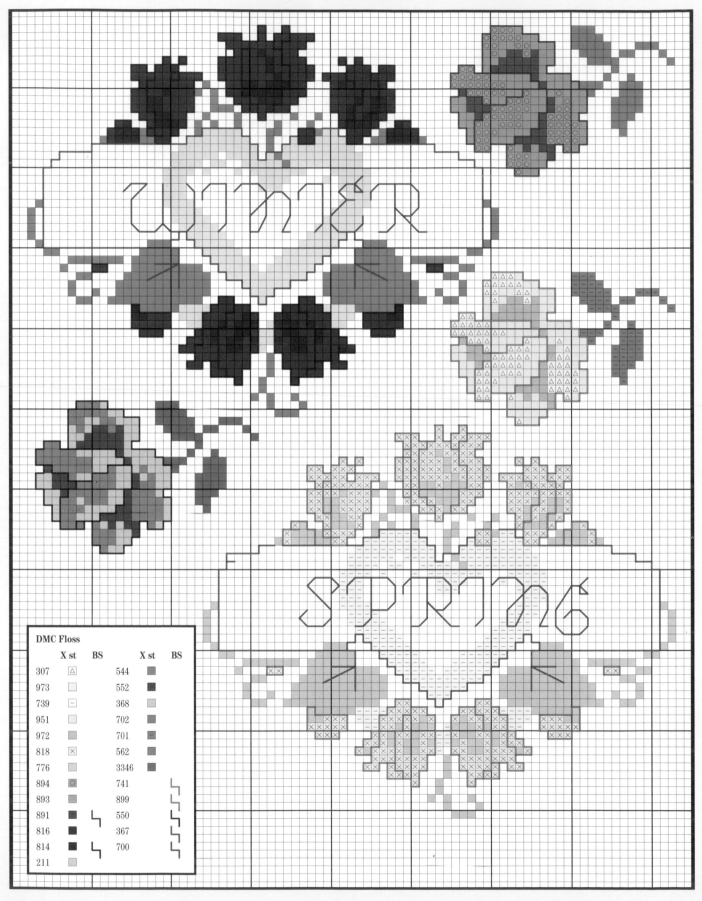

DMC Floss

	X st	BS		X st	BS
307			544		
973			552		
739			368		
951			702		
972			701		
818			562		
776			3346		
894			741		
893			899		
891			550		
816			367		
814			700		
211					

For All Seasons

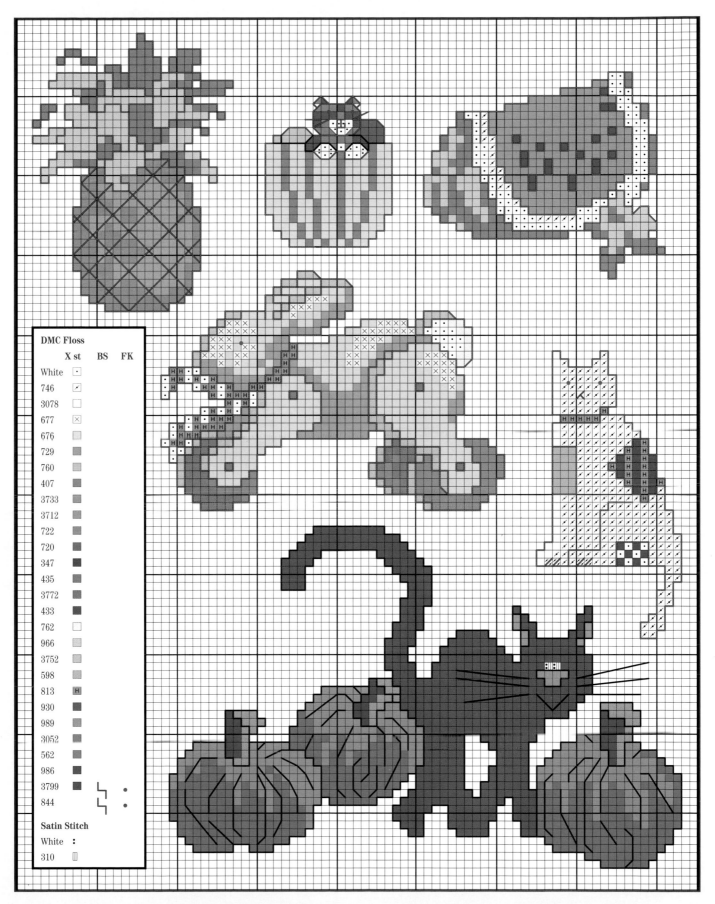

DMC Floss

	X st	BS	FK
White	·		
746	⁄		
3078	☐		
677	✕		
676			
729			
760			
407			
3733			
3712			
722			
720			
347			
435			
3772			
433			
762	☐		
966			
3752			
598			
813	H		
930			
989			
3052			
562			
986			
3799			
844			·

Satin Stitch

White	:
310	▨

For All Seasons

For All Seasons

DMC Floss

	X st		X st		X st	BS
Ecru	△	351	■	611	■	
727	□	350	■	3021	J	⌐
722	■	341	■	3033	□	
721	⧄	340	■	841	■	
818	□	772	□	610	▣	
353	⧄	3364	■	840	■	
3326	■	3032	■	720	■	⌐
899	+	988	■			

For All Seasons

DMC Floss		
	X st	BS
677		
745		
744		
725		
676	M	
729		
977		
740		
921		
347	V	⌐
326		
355		
816		⌐
353		
327		
3756	.	
800		
824		
311		⌐
371	U	⌐
3052		
910		
3345		
890	✳	
844		⌐
986		⌐
435		⌐

For All Seasons

DMC Floss

	X st	BS
White	·	
725		
743		
948		
754		
976		⌐
666		
347		
301	▲	
326	✳	
553		
3041		
928		
930		⌐
502		
912		
501		⌐
3053		
703		
701	✕	
699	◇	⌐
841		⌐
840		⌐
415		
414		⌐

For All Seasons

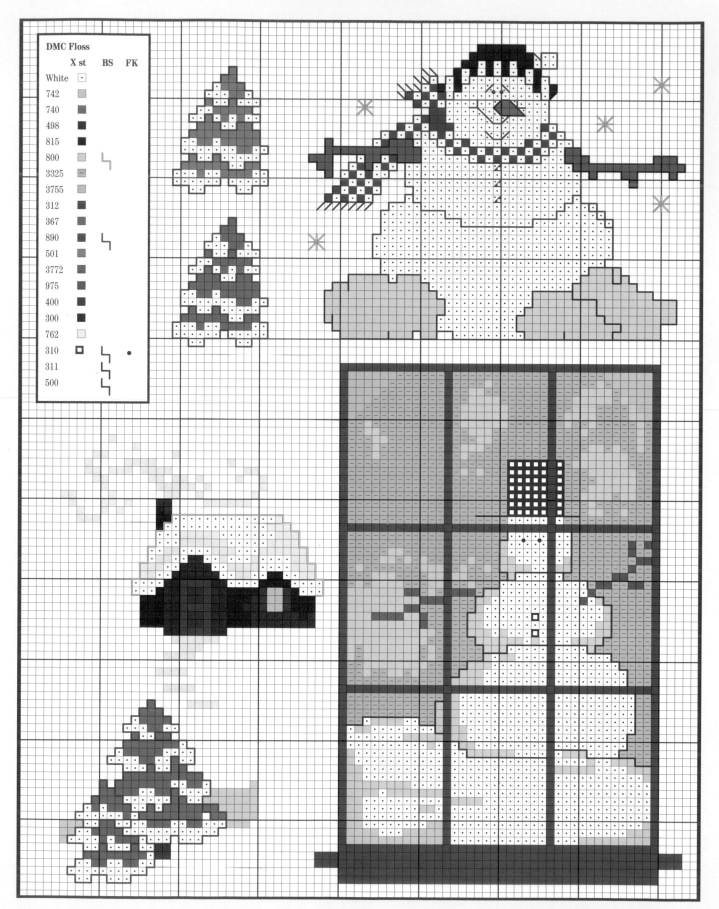

For All Seasons

DMC Floss

	X st	BS	FK
White	·		
725		⌐	
783			
721			
976			
975			
224			
223	∪		
221		⌐	
605			
3806	M		
3804			
3803		⌐	
932	⊠		
800			
320	▢		
367			
319			
910	⊠		
842			
841	⊡		
840	K	⌐	•
400			
839		⌐	
928			
927		⌐	
930			
3799		⌐	
890		⌐	
898		⌐	
3371		⌐	•

Criss Cross

605 & 3803		✕

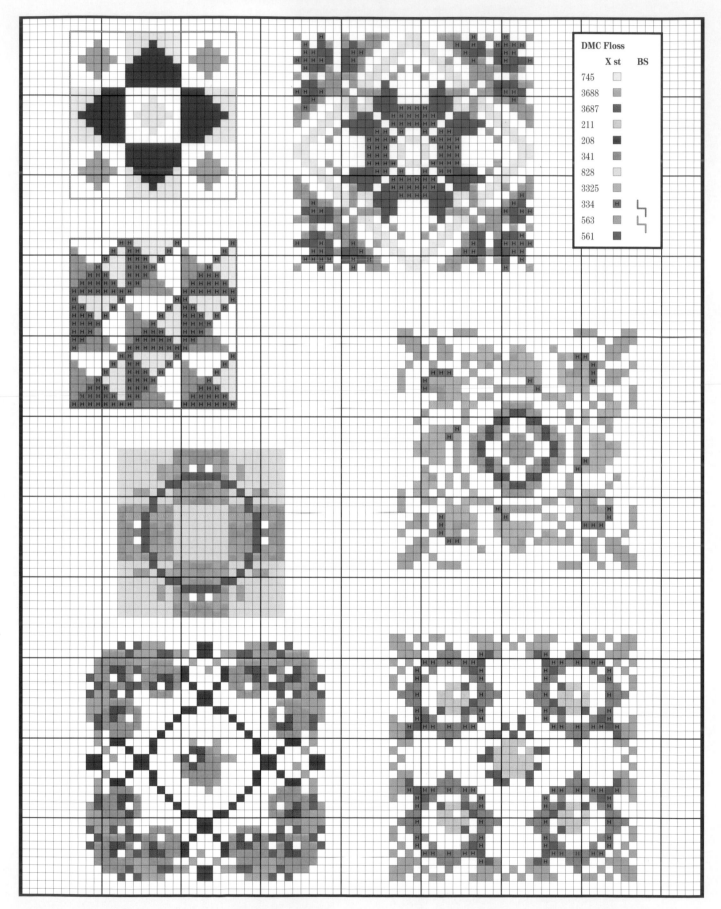

For All Seasons

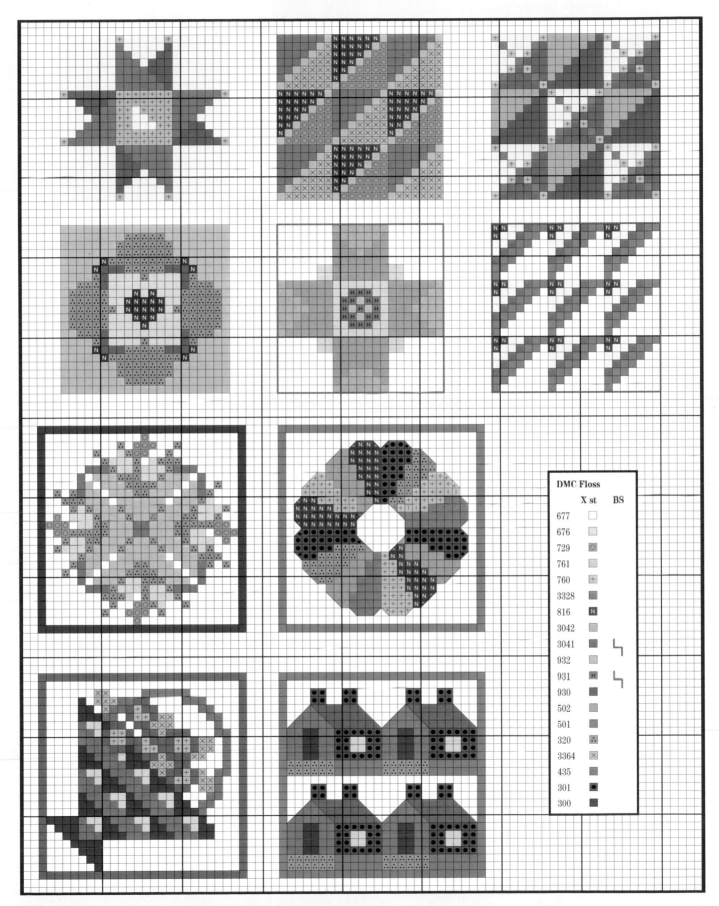

DMC Floss		
	X st	**BS**
677		
676		
729		
761		
760		
3328		
816	N	
3042		
3041		⌐
932		
931	H	⌐
930		
502		
501		
320		
3364	✕	
435		
301	●	
300		

Young at Heart

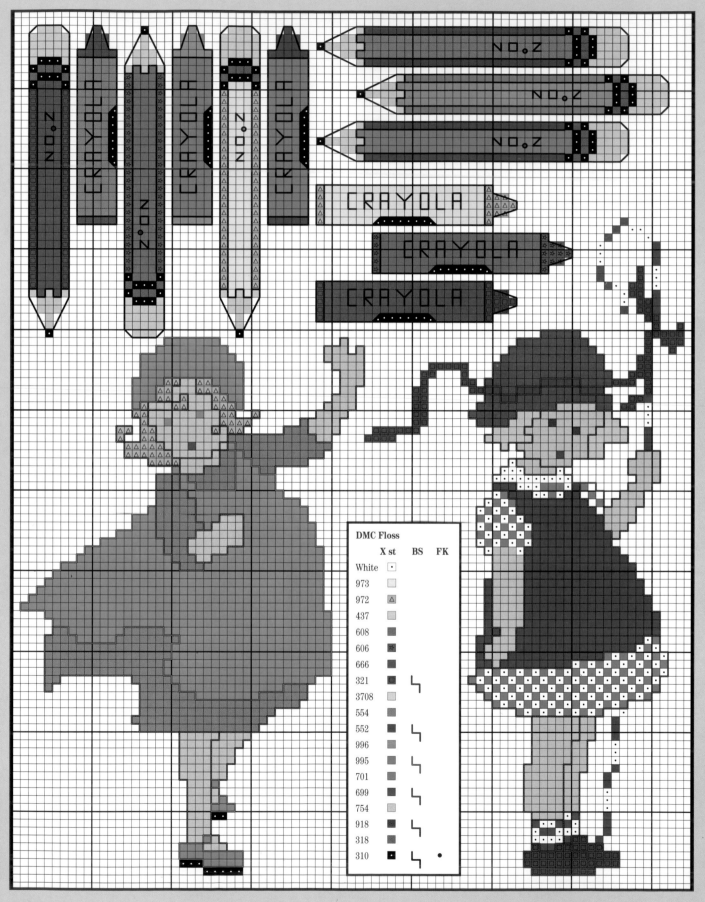

DMC Floss

	X st	BS	FK
White	·		
973			
972	△		
437			
608			
606	✳		
666			
321		⌐	
3708			
554			
552		⌐	
996		⌐	
995		⌐	
701			
699		⌐	
754			
918		⌐	
318			
310	·	⌐	•

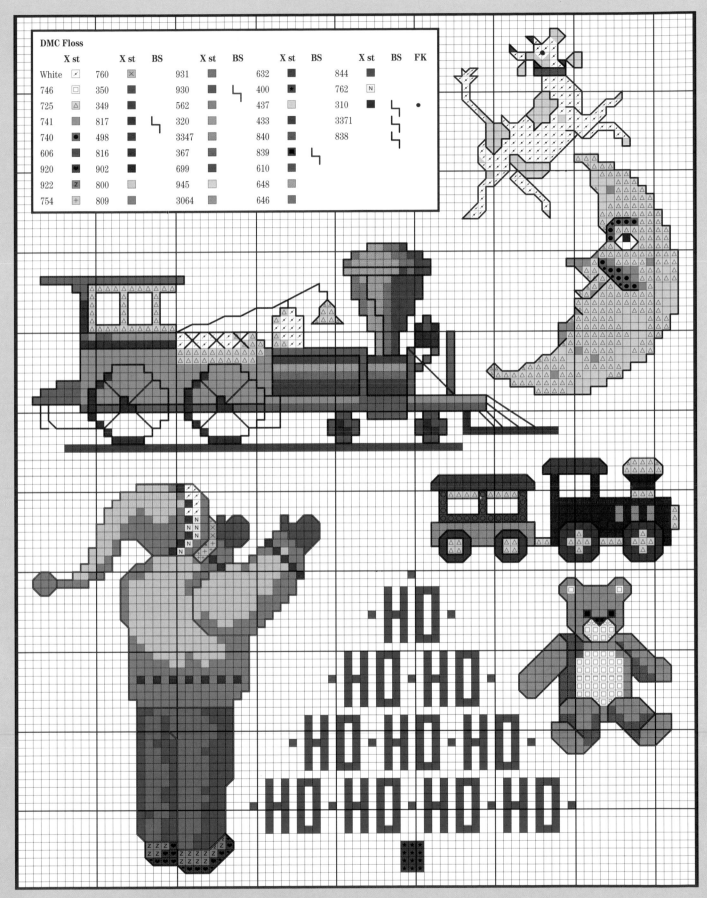

DMC Floss

X st		X st	BS	X st	BS	X st	BS	X st	BS	FK
White		760		931		632		844		
746		350		930		400		762		
725		349		562		437		310		•
741		817		320		433		3371		
740		498		3347		840		838		
606		816		367		839				
920		902		699		610				
922		800		945		648				
754		809		3064		646				

HO
HO·HO
HO·HO·HO
HO·HO·HO·HO

Young at Heart

DMC Floss

	X st		X st	BS	FK
White	·	930			
Ecru		928			
676		3364			
729	◉	367			
722		739			
721	▲	738			
720		754			
606		435			
921		301			
347		433			
760		918			
761		839			
894		801			
809		3023			
340		415			
932		310	·		●
931	★	844			●

DMC Floss

	X st	BS	FK
White	·		
744			
743	✕		
754			
356			
816			
666			
321			•
818			
776			
760			
304		⌐	
762			
928			
932			
955			
702			
700			
561		⌐	
699		⌐	
841			
3371		⌐	
931		⌐	
797		⌐	
311		⌐	
413		⌐	•
434		⌐	•
838		⌐	
310			•

Young at Heart

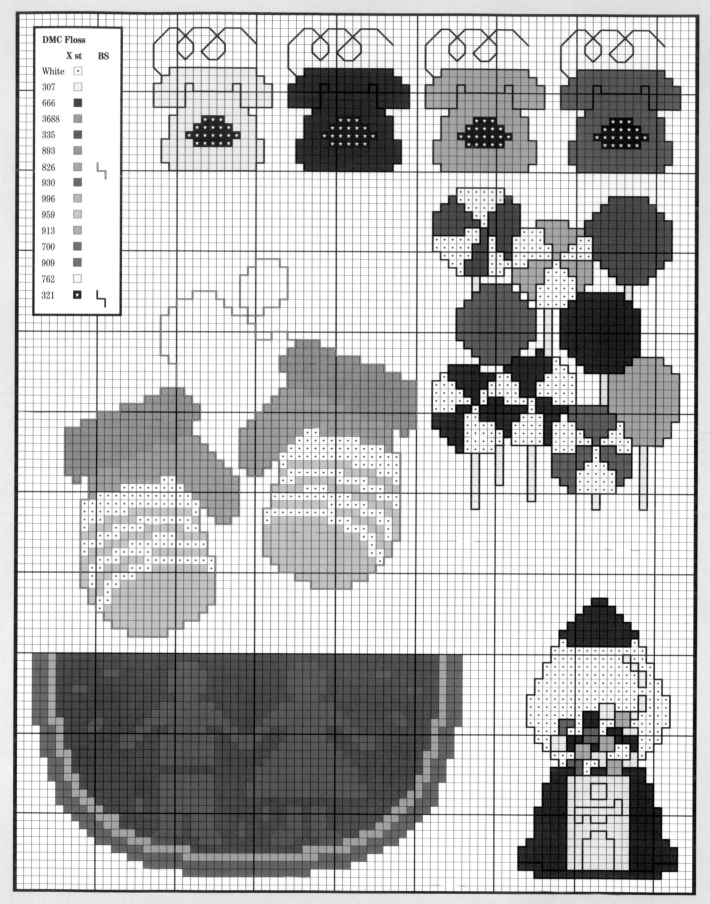

DMC Floss		
	X st	BS
White	·	
307		
666		
3688		
335		
893		
826		⌐
930		
996		
959		
913		
700		
909		
762		⌐
321	★	⌐

Young at Heart

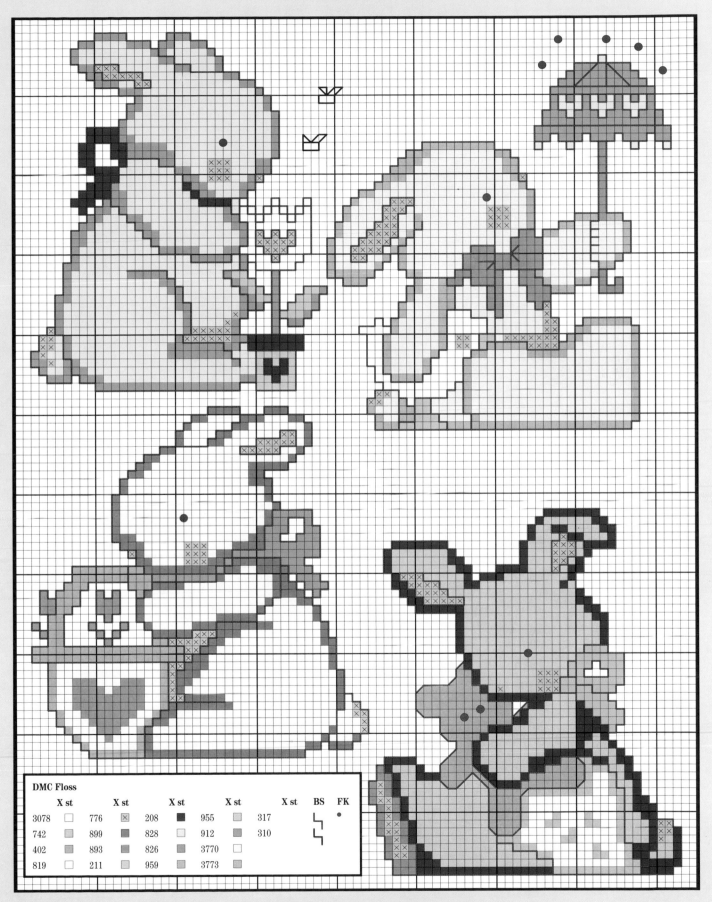

DMC Floss									
X st		**X st**		**X st**		**X st**		**X st**	**BS** **FK**
3078		776		208		955		317	
742		899		828		912		310	
402		893		826		3770			
819		211		959		3773			

DMC Floss

	X st		X st		X st		X st		X st	BS	FK
White	·	945		3756		926		844			
677		3779	H	3761	△	3052		3799			●
676	✗	3773	○	3766		436					
729		3712		813		434					
3774		347		928	□	648					

Young at Heart

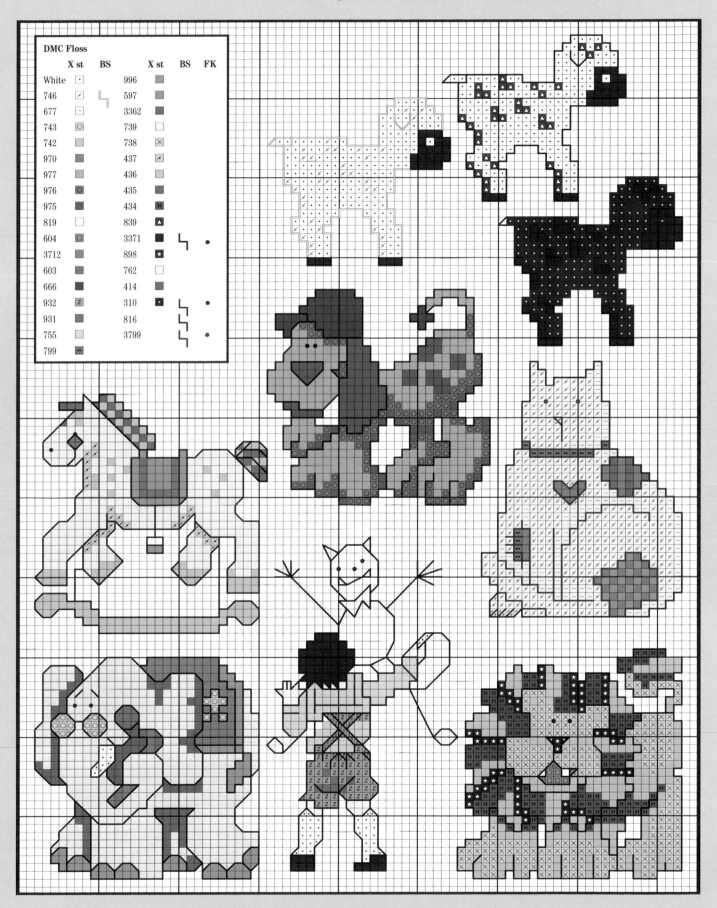

DMC Floss

	X st		X st	BS
746		913		
945		909		
727		3829		
326		433		
794		451		
3807		310		

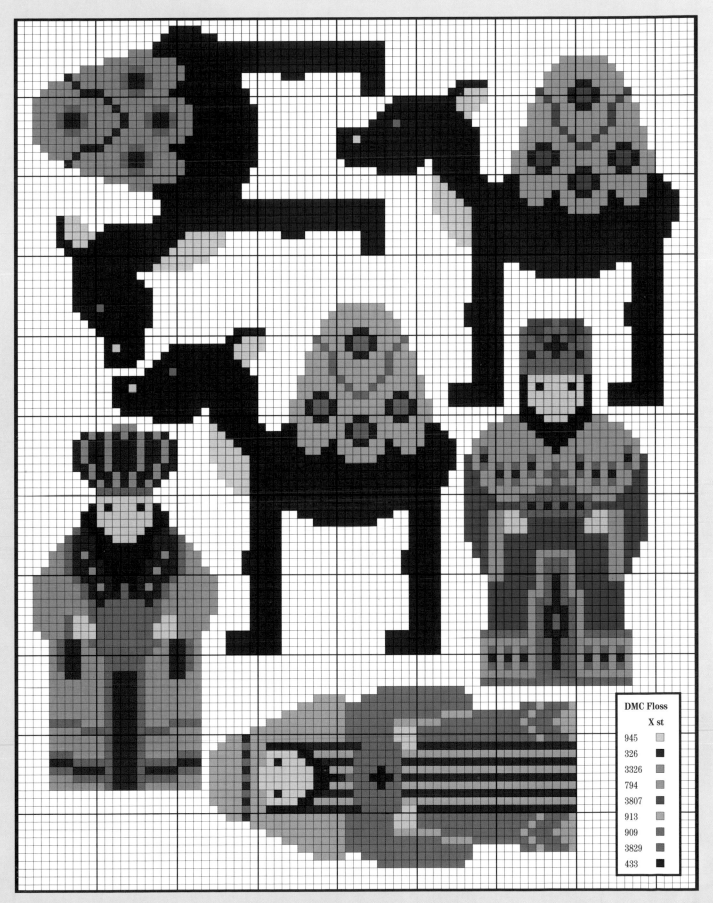

DMC Floss X st	
945	
326	
3326	
794	
3807	
913	
909	
3829	
433	

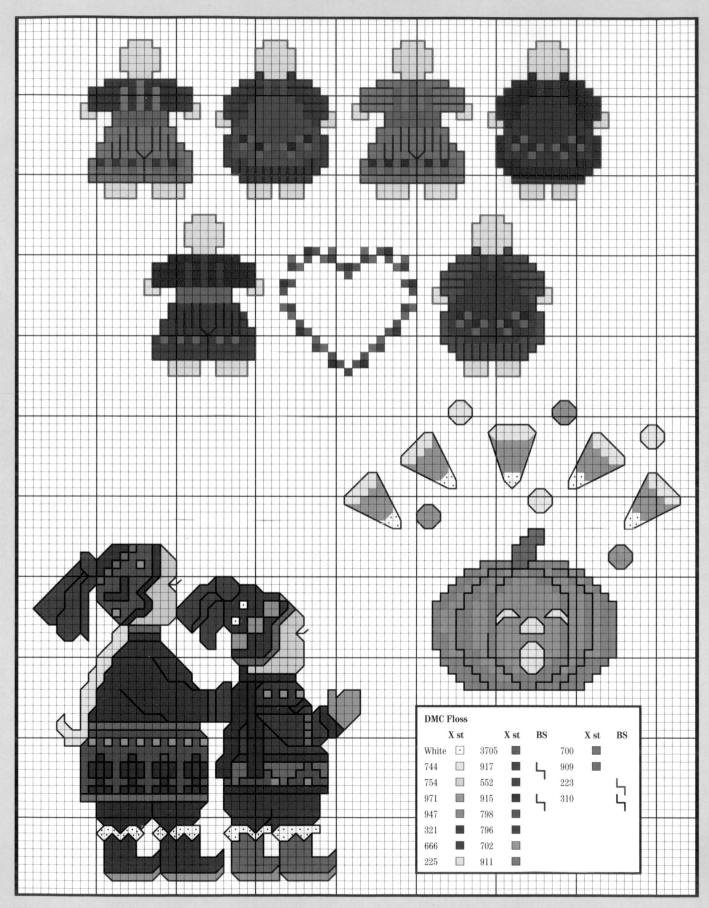

DMC Floss

	X st		X st	BS		X st	BS
White	⊡	3705			700		
744		917		⌐	909		
754		552			223		⌐
971		915		⌐	310		⌐
947		798					
321		796					
666		702					
225		911					

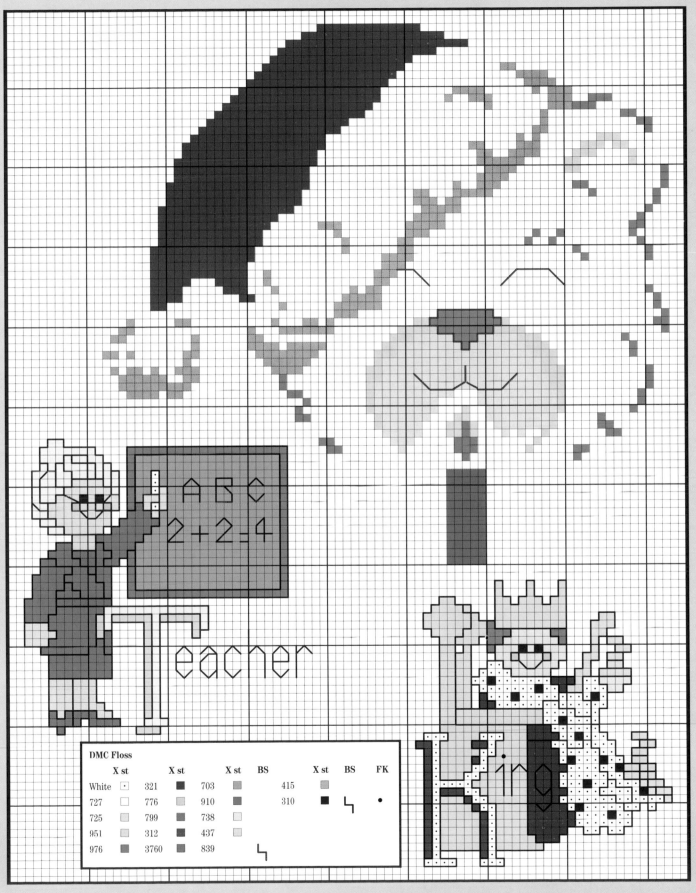

DMC Floss

X st		X st		X st		BS		X st	BS	FK
White	·	321	■	703	■	415	■			
727	□	776	■	910	■	310		■	⌐	•
725	■	799	■	738	□					
951	■	312	■	437	■					
976	■	3760	■	839	■	⌐				

DMC Floss

	X st		X st		X st	BS	FK
White	·	321	■	703	▨		
727		971	▨	701	▨		
725	▨	976	▨	415	▨		
951		3760	▨	300	■		
776	▨	312	■	310	■	⌐	•

Doctor

Gardener

Painter

Lion tamer

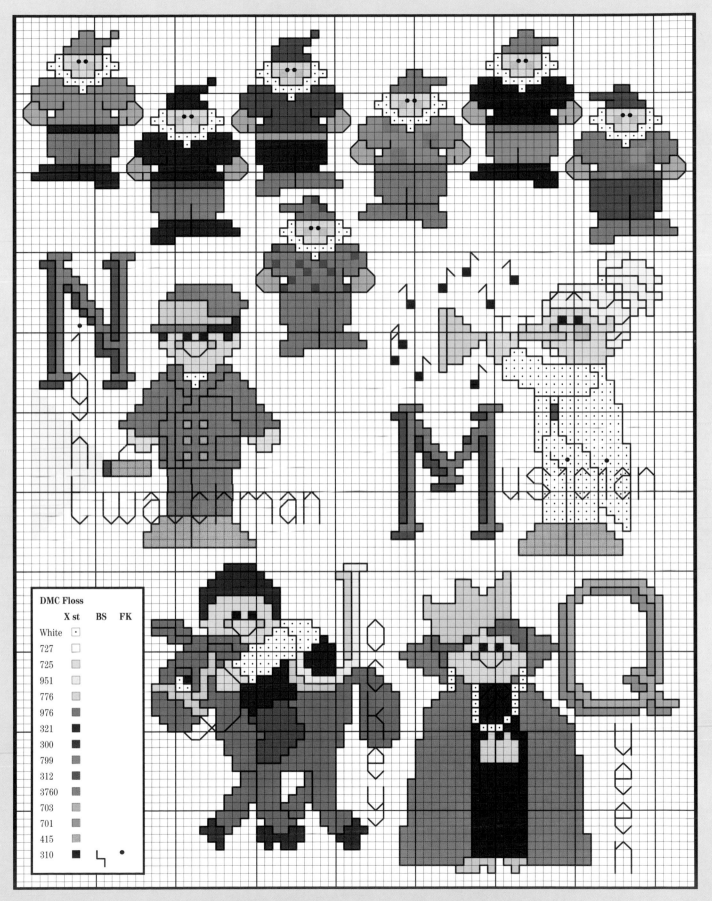

Young at Heart

Code for pages 60–61.

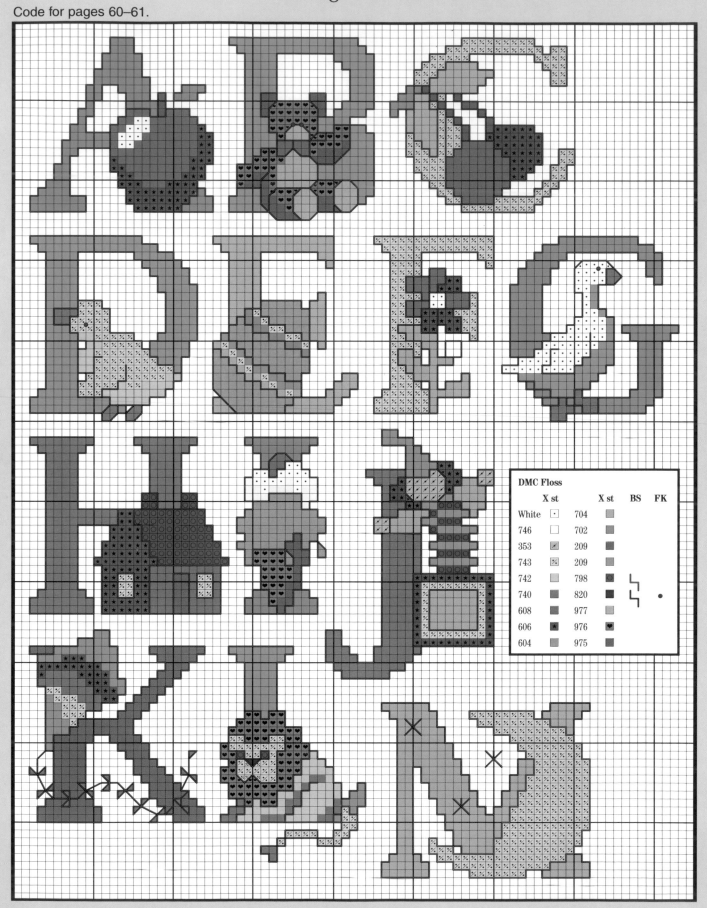

DMC Floss

	X st		X st	BS	FK
White	·	704			
746		702			
353		209			
743		209			
742		798			
740		820			
608		977			
606	★	976	♥		
604		975			

Young at Heart

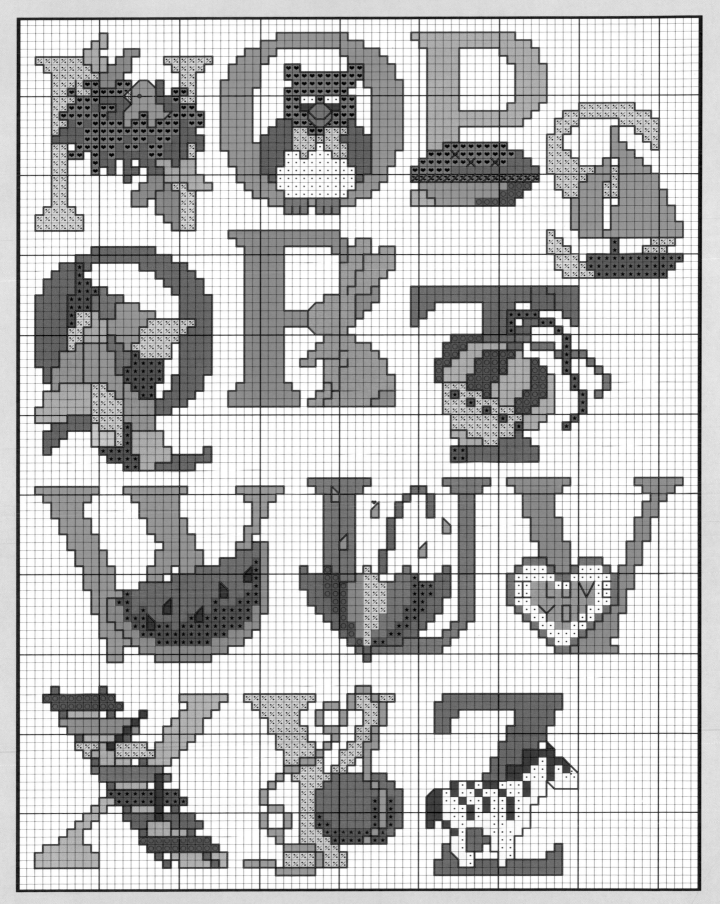

Creatures Great & Small

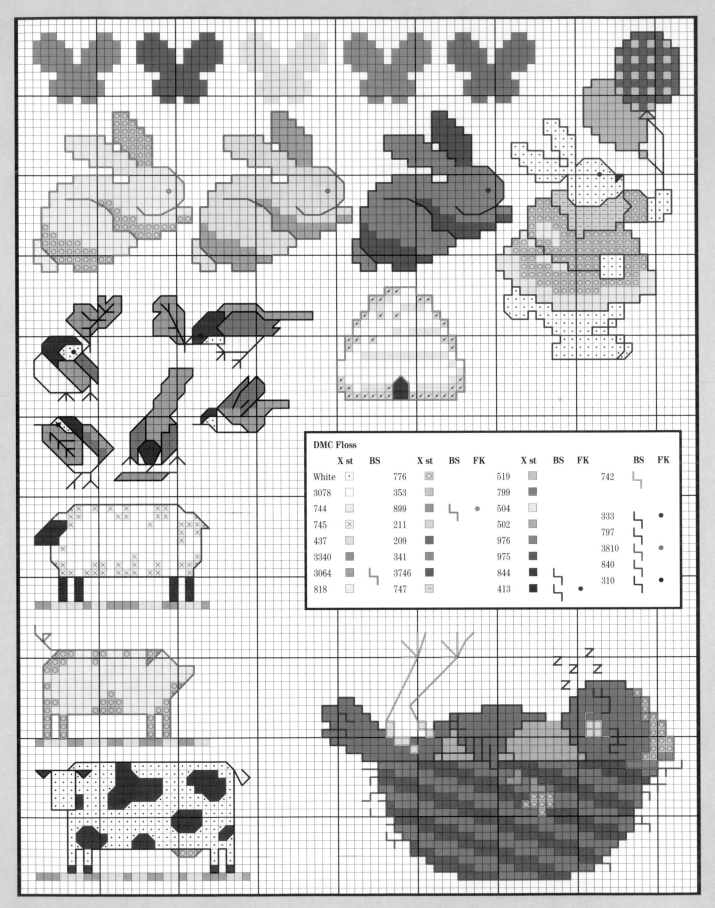

DMC Floss

	X st	BS		X st	BS	FK		X st	BS	FK		BS	FK
White			776				519				742		
3078			353				799						
744			899				504				333		
745			211				502				797		
437			209				976				3810		
3340			341				975				840		
3064			3746				844				310		
818			747				413						

Creatures Great & Small

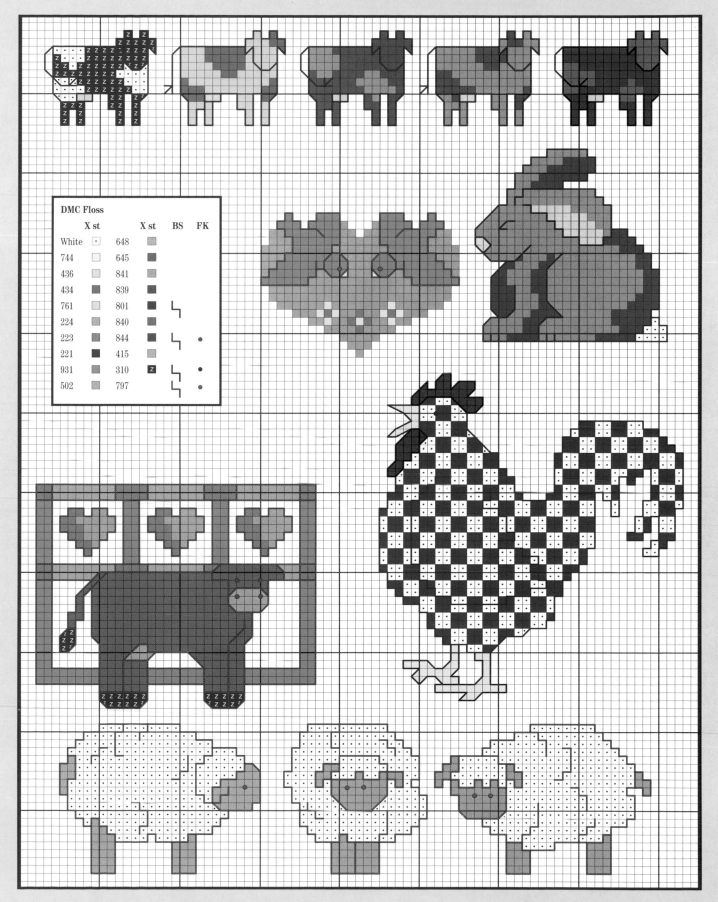

DMC Floss

	X st		X st	BS	FK
White	·	648			
744		645			
436		841			
434		839			
761		801		⌐	
224		840			
223		844		⌐	•
221		415			
931		310	Z	⌐	•
502		797		⌐	•

Creatures Great & Small

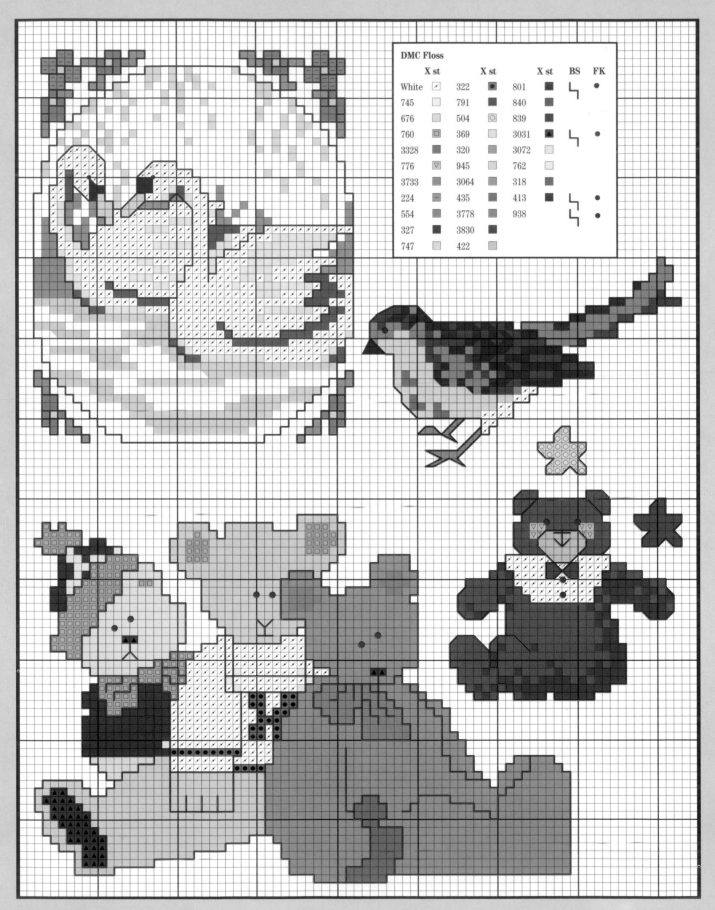

DMC Floss

	X st		X st		X st	BS	FK
White		322		801			●
745		791		840			
676		504		839			
760		369		3031			●
3328		320		3072			
776		945		762			
3733		3064		318			
224		435		413			●
554		3778		938			●
327		3830					
747		422					

Creatures Great & Small

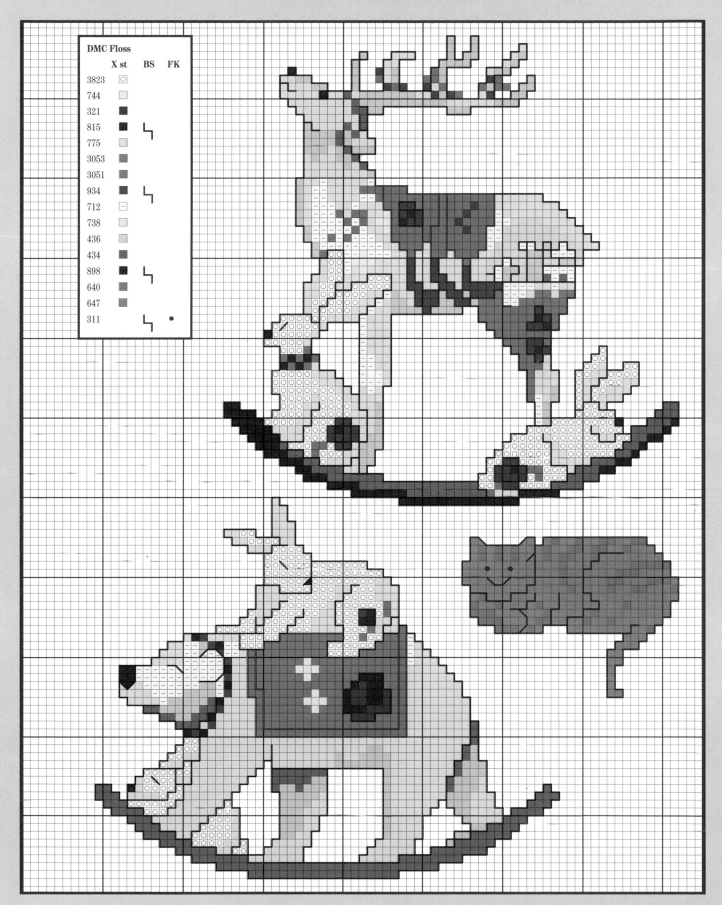

DMC Floss

	X st	BS	FK
3823	⊙		
744			
321			
815		⌐	
775			
3053			
3051			
934		⌐	
712	−		
738			
436			
434			
898		⌐	
640			
647			
311		⌐	●

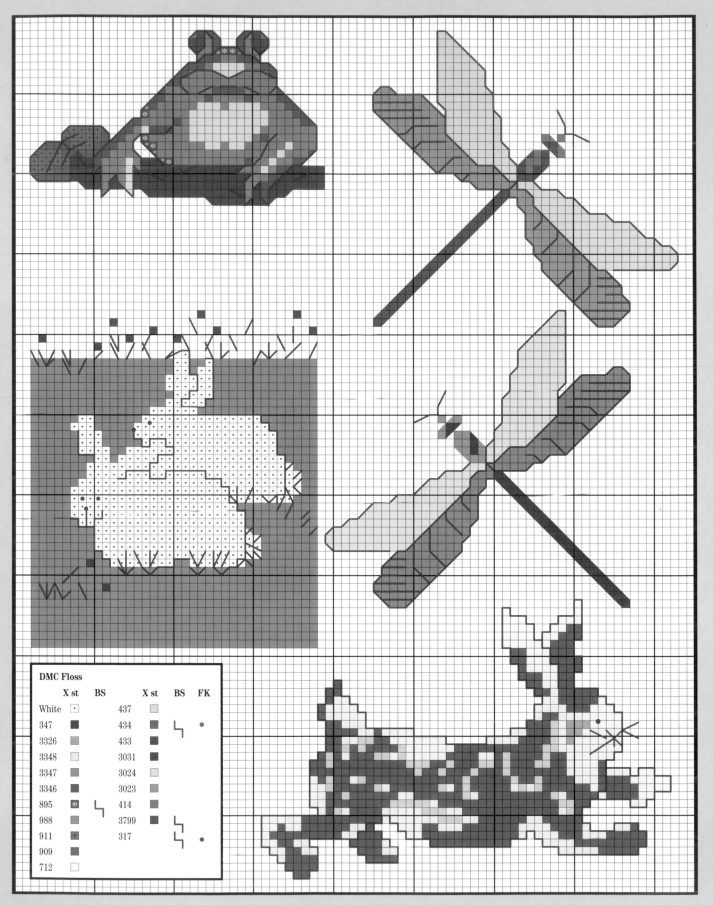

DMC Floss

	X st	BS		X st	BS	FK
White	·		437			
347			434		⌐	•
3326			433			
3348			3031			
3347			3024			
3346			3023			
895	✳	⌐	414			
988			3799		⌐	
911	+		317		⌐	•
909						
712						

Creatures Great & Small

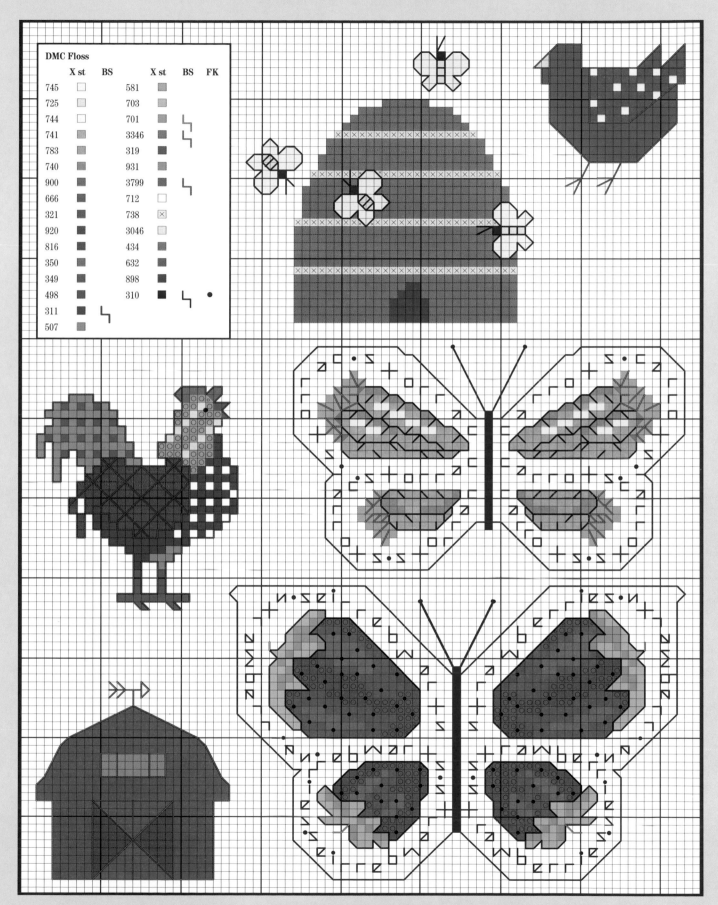

DMC Floss

	X st	BS		X st	BS	FK
745			581			
725			703			
744			701		⌐	
741			3346		⌐	
783			319			
740			931			
900			3799		⌐	
666			712			
321			738	⊠		
920			3046			
816			434			
350			632			
349			898			
498			310		⌐	●
311		⌐				
507						

DMC Floss

	X st	BS		X st	BS		X st	BS	FK
White	·		829			841			
727			951			839			
725			407			838		⌐	
740			632			317		⌐	•
352			3776			413			
761	⊚		739			3799		⌐	•
747			437		⌐	311		⌐	•
519			435	S					
3347		⌐	434						
833			433						
831	N		801		⌐				

Creatures Great & Small

DMC Floss

	X st		X st		X st	BS	FK
729	■	319	■	840	■		
3776	■	680	■	839	■		
3777	■	3064	■	3799	■	┘	
319	■	712	□	489			●
336	■	613	■				
500	■	611	■				

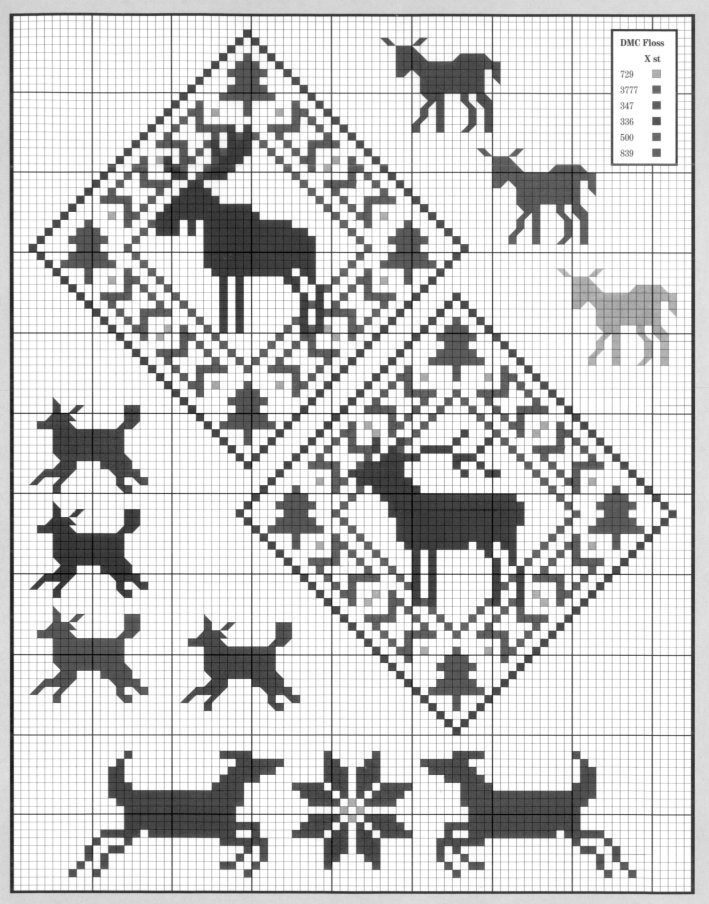

Creatures Great & Small

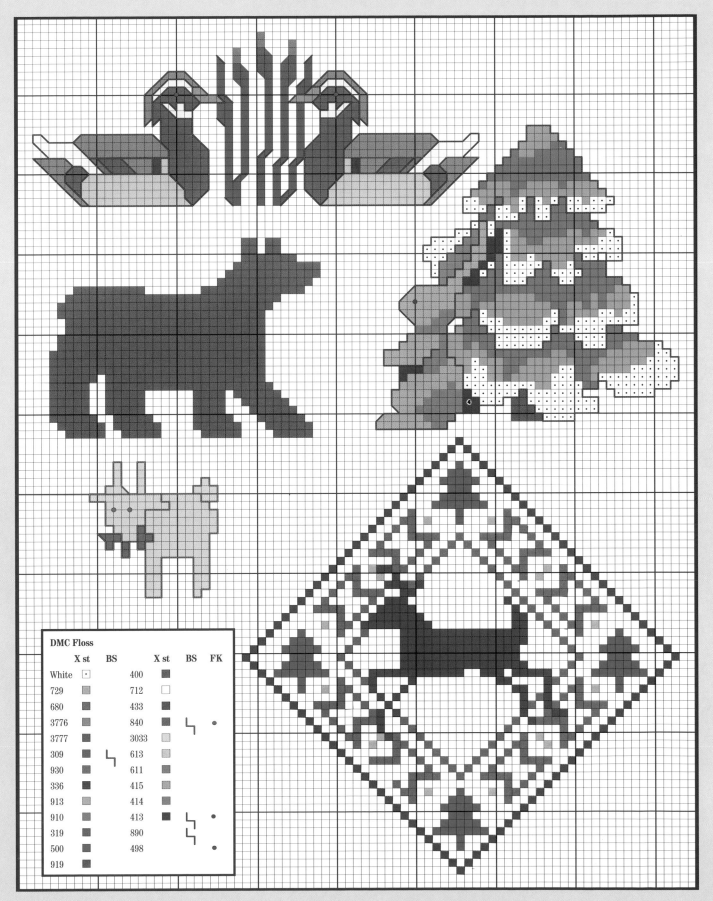

DMC Floss

	X st	BS		X st	BS	FK
White	·		400	▓		
729	▓		712	☐		
680	▓		433	▓		
3776	▓		840	▓	⌐	•
3777	▓		3033	▓		
309	▓	⌐	613	▓		
930	▓		611	▓		
336	▓		415	▓		
913	▓		414	▓		
910	▓		413	▓	⌐	•
319	▓		890		⌐	
500	▓		498			•
919	▓					

Creatures Great & Small

DMC Floss

	X st	BS	FK
White	·		
746	⊠		
677	▫		
676	◪		
729	▪		
3774	▪		
945	▪		
436	▪		
3712	▪		
347	▪		
434	▪		
3756	◪		
3761	▪		
928	▫		
966	○		
598	▪		
597	△		
813	H		
799	J		
932	▪		
930	▪		
926	▪		
3052	▪		
3362	▪		
844	▪		
3799		⌐	●

DMC Floss

	X st		X st	BS	FK
White	·	400			
677		436			
3776		434			
3328		433			
666		840			
304		839		⌐	
597		838			•
991		415			
632		3371		⌐	
407		310			

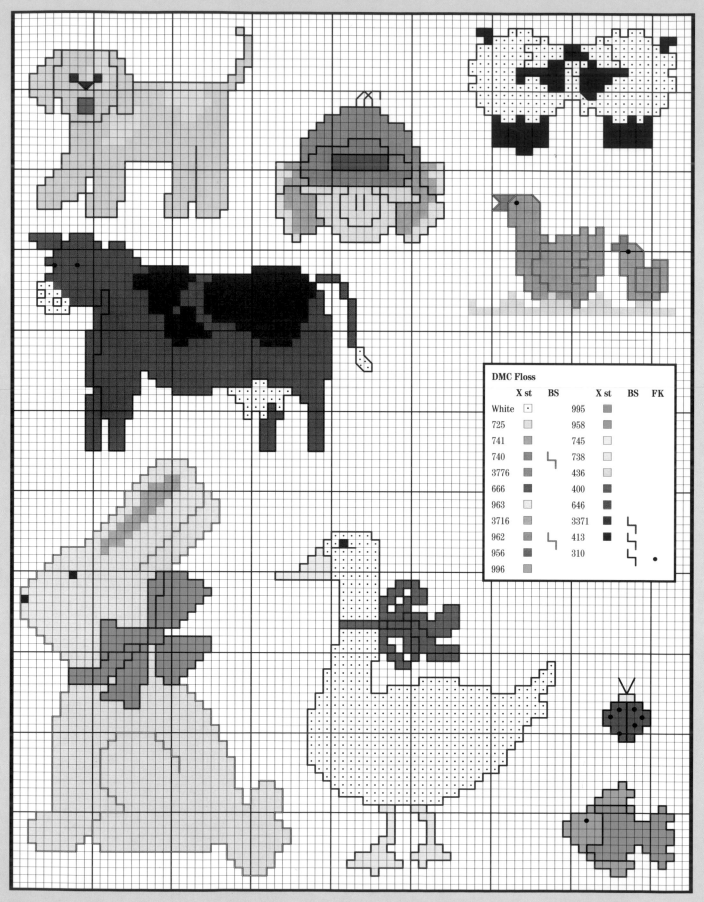

DMC Floss

	X st	BS		X st	BS	FK
White	·		995			
725			958			
741			745			
740		⌐	738			
3776			436			
666			400			
963			646			
3716			3371		⌐	
962		⌐	413		⌐	
956			310		⌐	•
996						

Creatures Great & Small

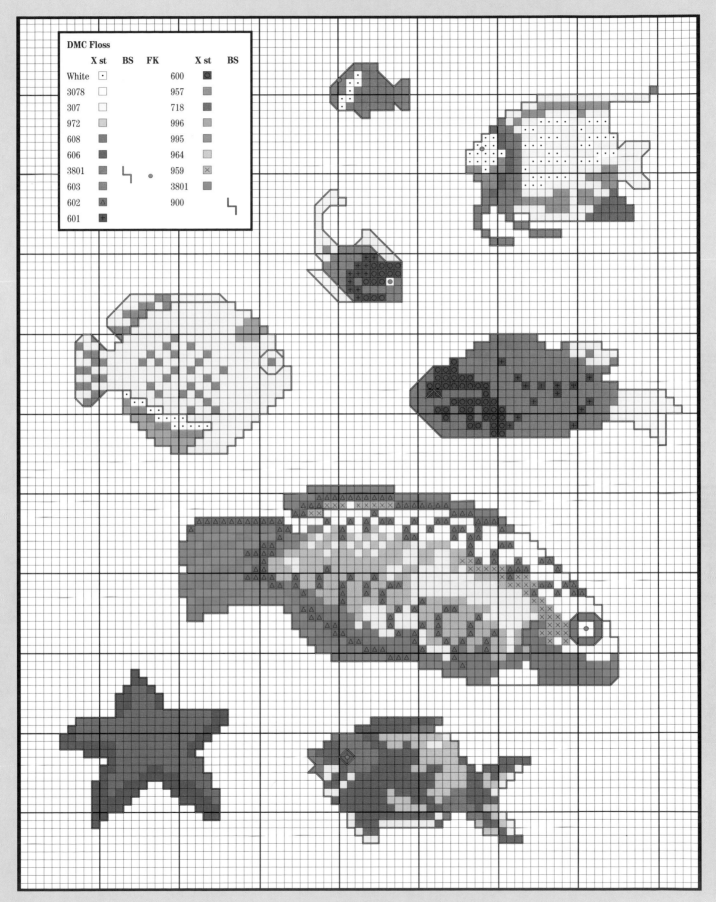

All Through the Year

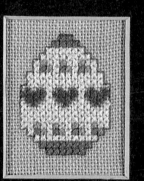

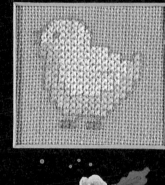

Happy Birthday

PURR-FECT PAIR

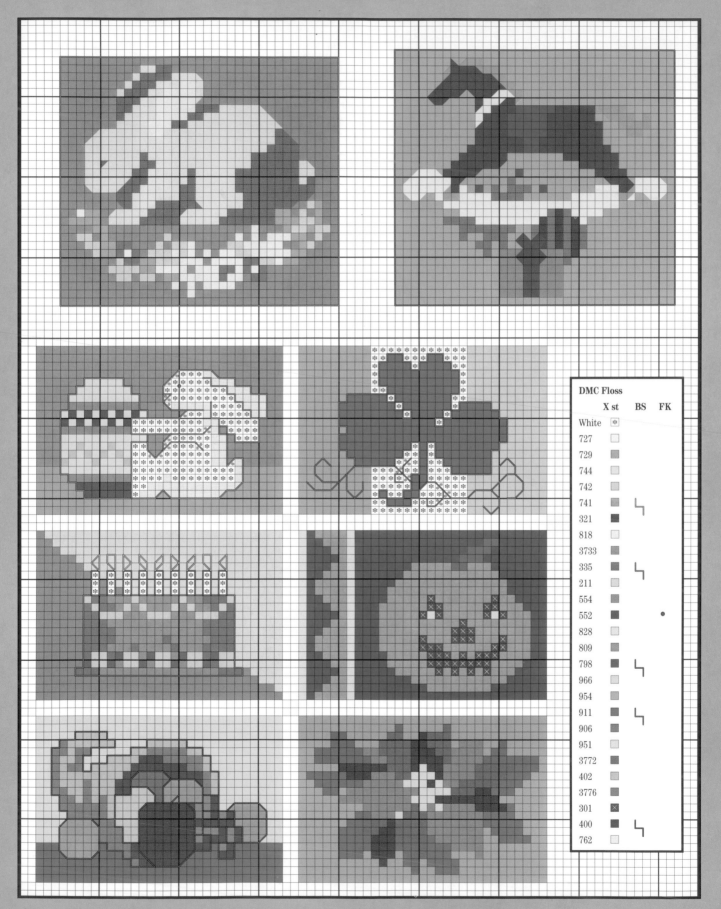

DMC Floss

	X st	BS	FK
White	✳		
727	⬜		
729	⬜		
744	⬜		
742	⬜		
741	⬜	⌐	
321	⬛		
818	⬜		
3733	⬜		
335	⬜	⌐	
211	⬜		
554	⬜		
552	⬛		●
828	⬜		
809	⬜		
798	⬜	⌐	
966	⬜		
954	⬜		
911	⬜	⌐	
906	⬜		
951	⬜		
3772	⬜		
402	⬜		
3776	⬜		
301	⨯		
400	⬛	⌐	
762	⬜		

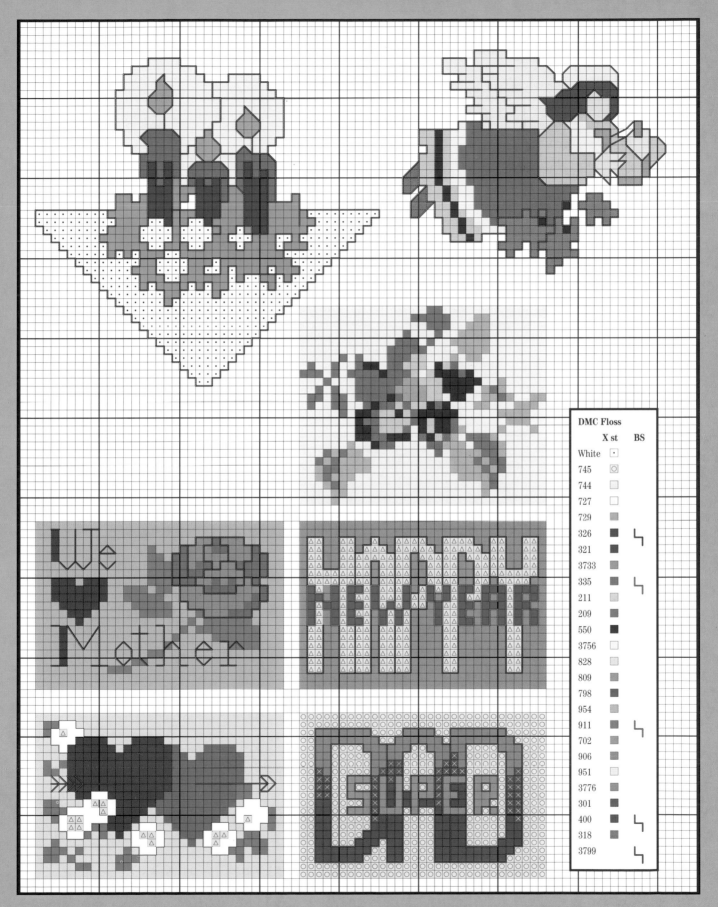

DMC Floss

	X st	BS
White	·	
745	⊚	
744		
727		
729		
326		⌐
321		
3733		
335		⌐
211		
209		
550		
3756		
828		
809		
798		
954		
911		⌐
702		
906		
951		
3776		
301		
400		⌐
318		
3799		⌐

DMC Floss

X st		X st		BS	FK		X st		BS	FK
754		899				368				
3776		335		⌐	●	367				
818		603				319		⌐		
353		304		⌐		310		⌐	●	
3326		553								

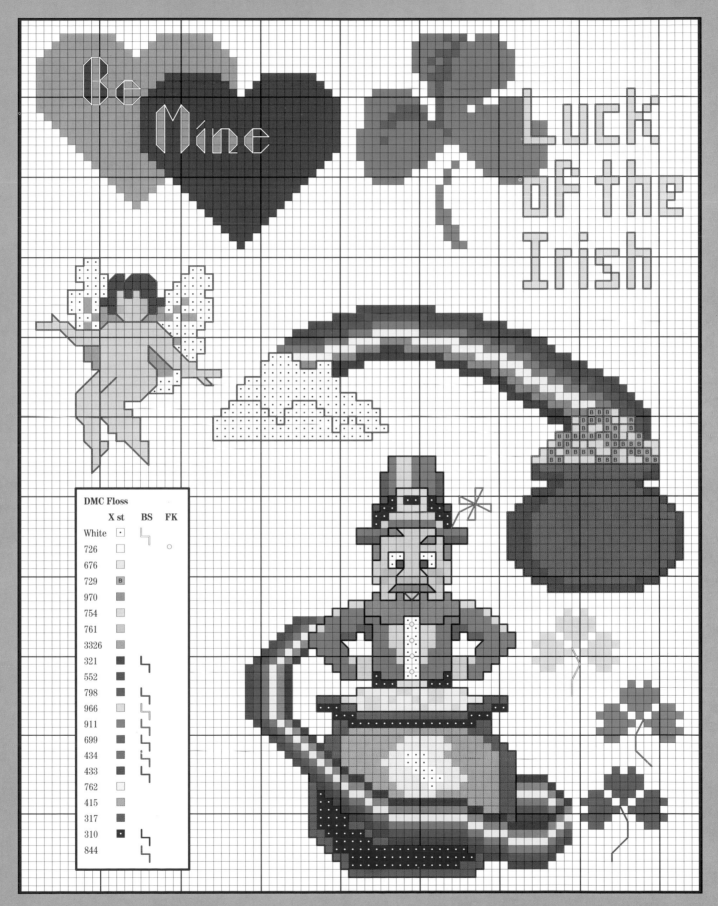

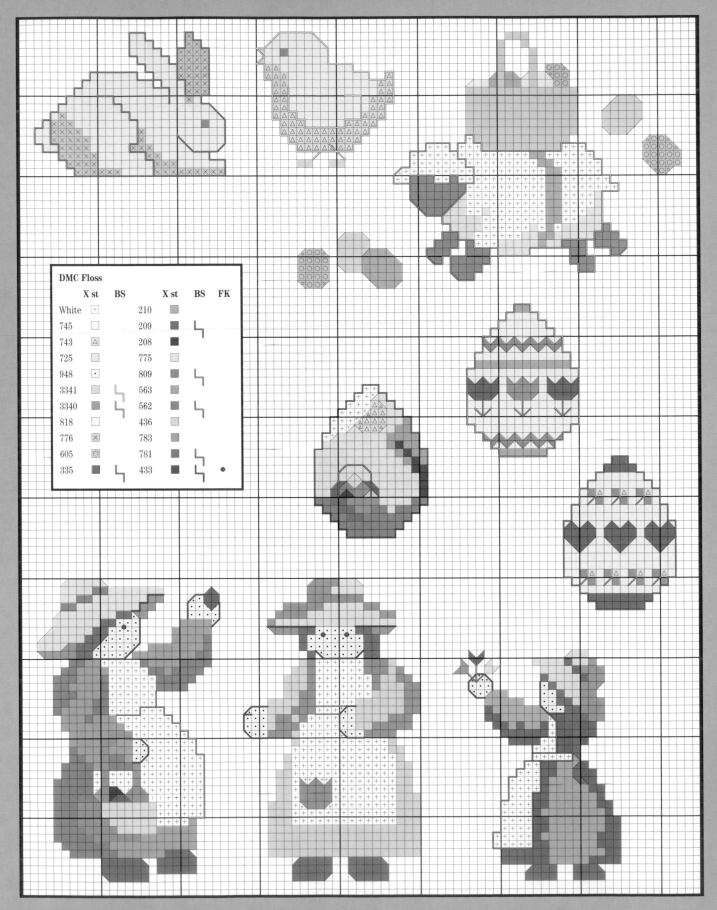

DMC Floss

	X st	BS		X st	BS	FK
White	+		210			
745			209		⌐	
743	△		208		⌐	
725			775			
948	·		809		⌐	
3341		⌐	563			
3340		⌐	562		⌐	
818			436			
776	X		783			
605	⌐		781		⌐	
335		⌐	433		⌐	●

DMC Floss						
	X st	BS	FK	X st	BS	FK
White	·			208		
742				995		·
725				796		
754				704		
740				701		
606				3064		
602				840		
601			·	310		·

prince
For A Day

Happy Birthday

princess
For A Day

Queen
For A Day

King
For A Day

DMC Floss

	X st	BS		X st		X st	BS
White	+		349		3345		
745			3687		402		
725		⌐	553		3776		
754			327		301		⌐
722			772		975		⌐
721	▲		907		3799		⌐
720			988		310	▨	⌐
352							

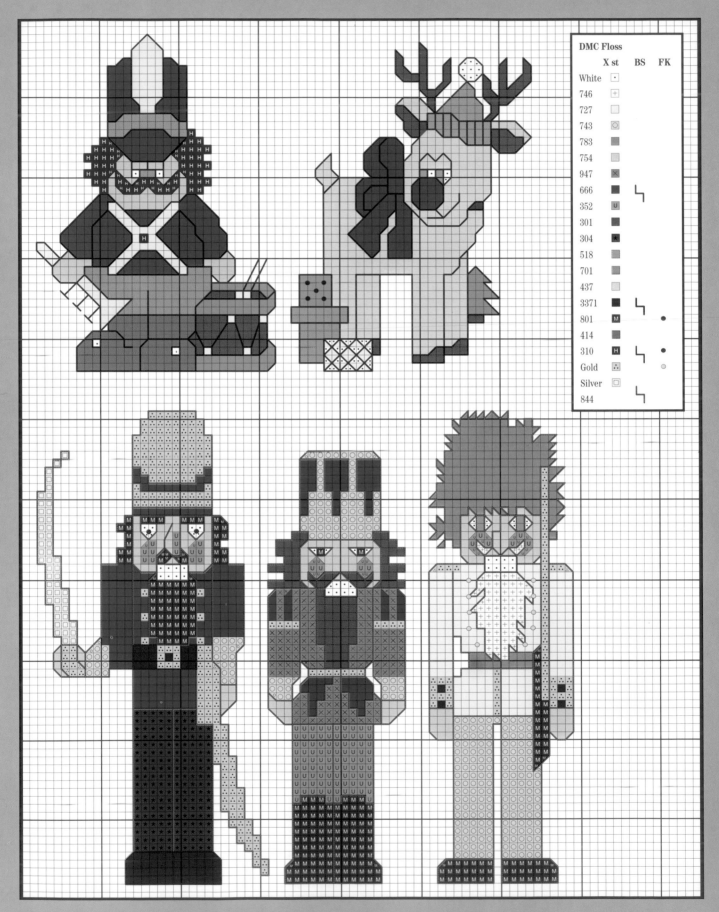

DMC Floss			
	X st	BS	FK
White	·		
746	+		
727			
743	⊙		
783	■		
754			
947	✕		
666	■	⌐	
352	U		
301	■		
304	★		
518	■		
701	■		
437			
3371	■	⌐	•
801	M		•
414	■		
310	H	⌐	•
Gold	⋰		○
Silver	▫	⌐	
844			

DMC Floss

	X st	BS		X st	BS	FK
White	·		334		⌐	•
743			792			
729		⌐	368			
754		⌐	989		⌐	•
740			986			
349			762			
498		⌐	414			
3731			844		⌐	
3687			552		⌐	•
554						

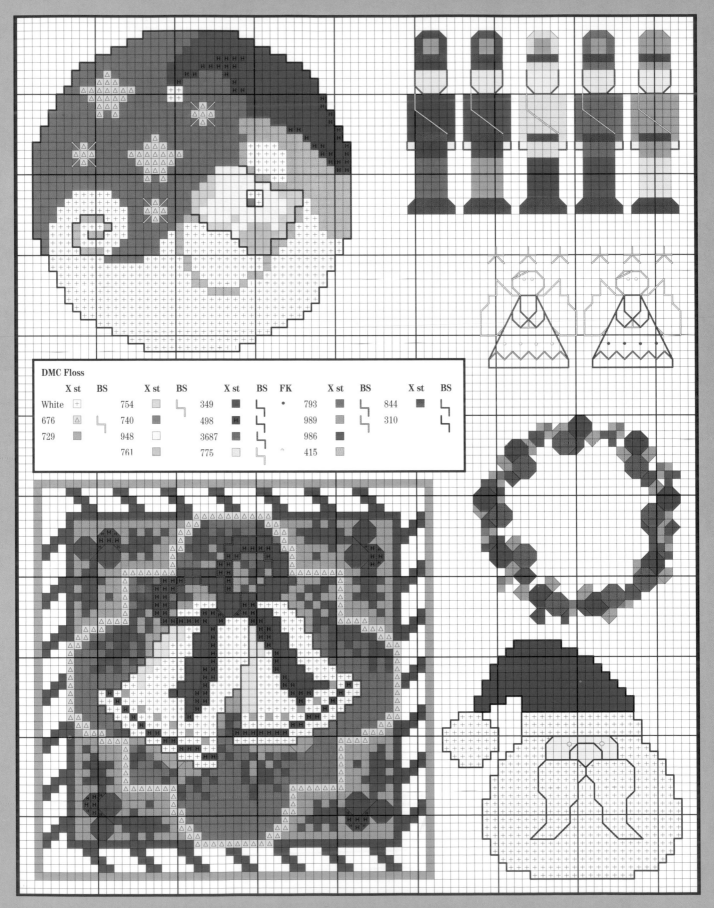

DMC Floss

	X st	BS		X st	BS		X st	BS	FK		X st	BS		X st	BS
White	+		754		⌐	349	■	⌐	•	793	■	⌐	844	■	⌐
676	△	⌐	740	■		498	H	⌐		989	■	⌐	310		⌐
729	■		948	□		3687	■	⌐	○	986	■				
			761	■		775	□	⌐		415	■				

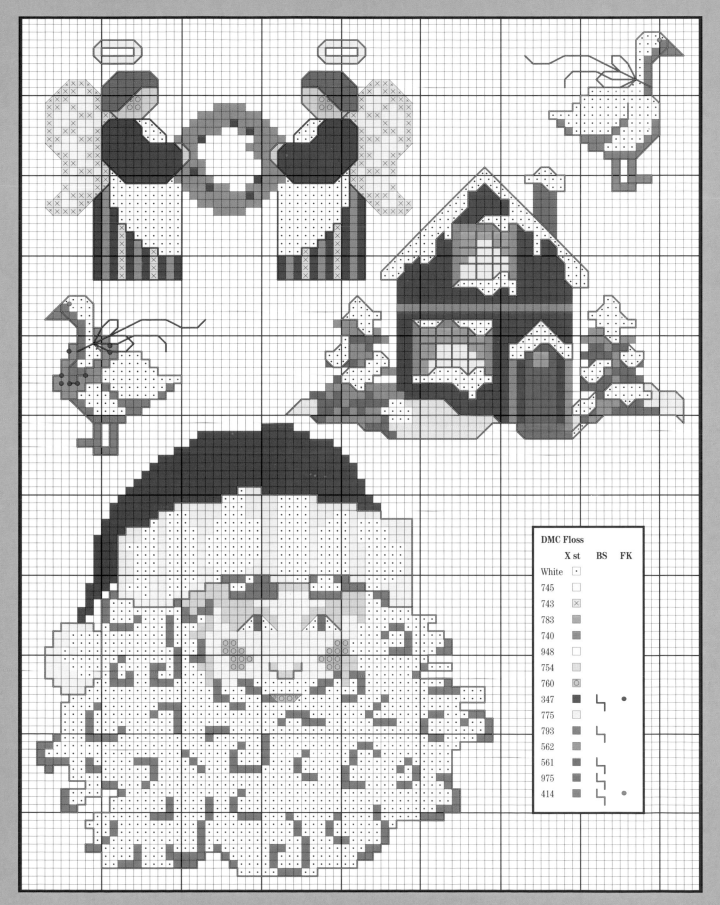

DMC Floss

	X st	BS	FK
White	·		
745			
743	⊠		
783			
740			
948			
754			
760	⊚		
347		⌐	•
775			
793		⌐	
562			
561		⌐	
975		⌐	
414		⌐	•

All Through the Year

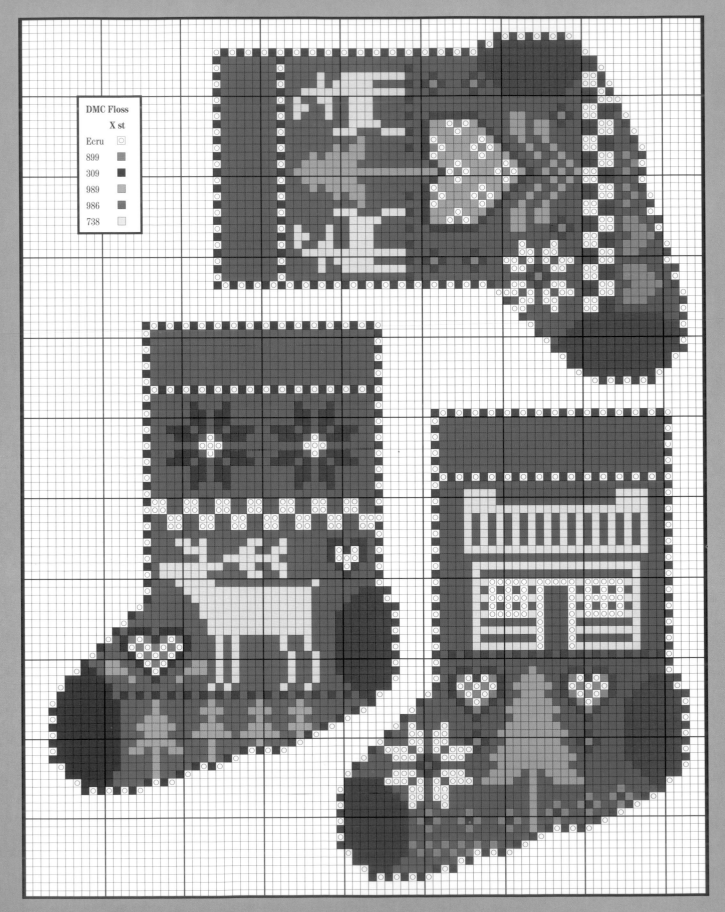

DMC Floss

	X st	BS		X st	BS
676			312		⌐
948			987		
761	⊙		890		
776			368		
3733			436		
3350		⌐	434		⌐
498			911		⌐
3753			814		⌐
3755					

Merry Christmas

WARM HANDS
WARM HEART

Bearly An Angel

NOEL

Cats have PURR sonality.

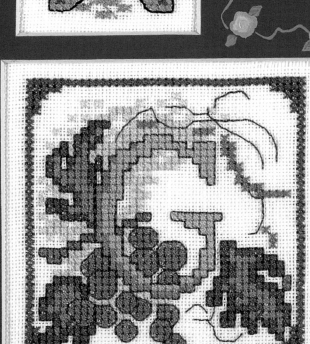

Alphabets & Sayings

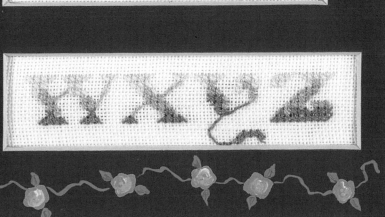

Code for pages 98–104.

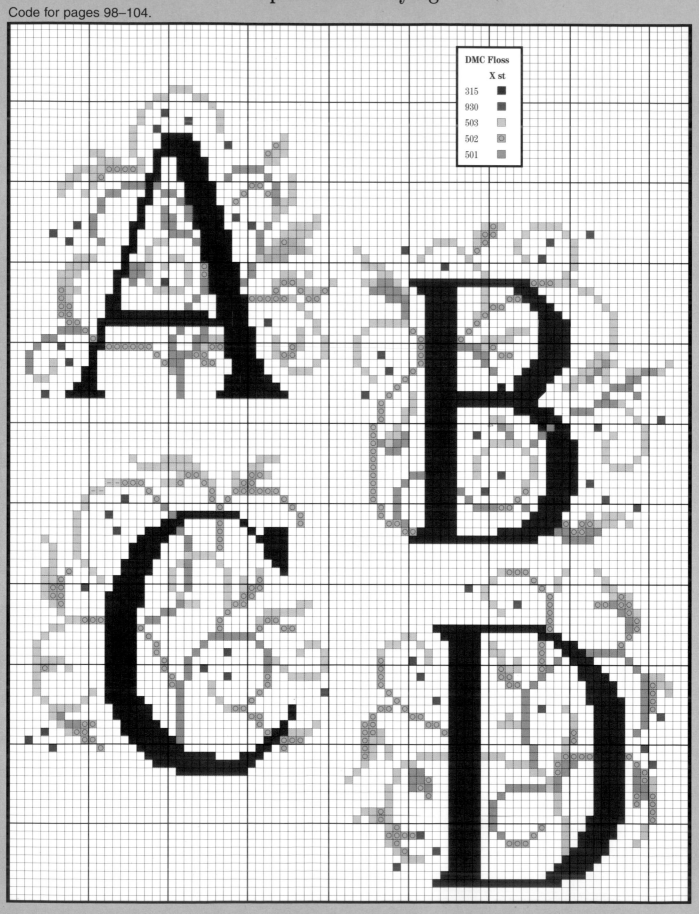

DMC Floss

X st

315	■
930	■
503	▨
502	⊙
501	▨

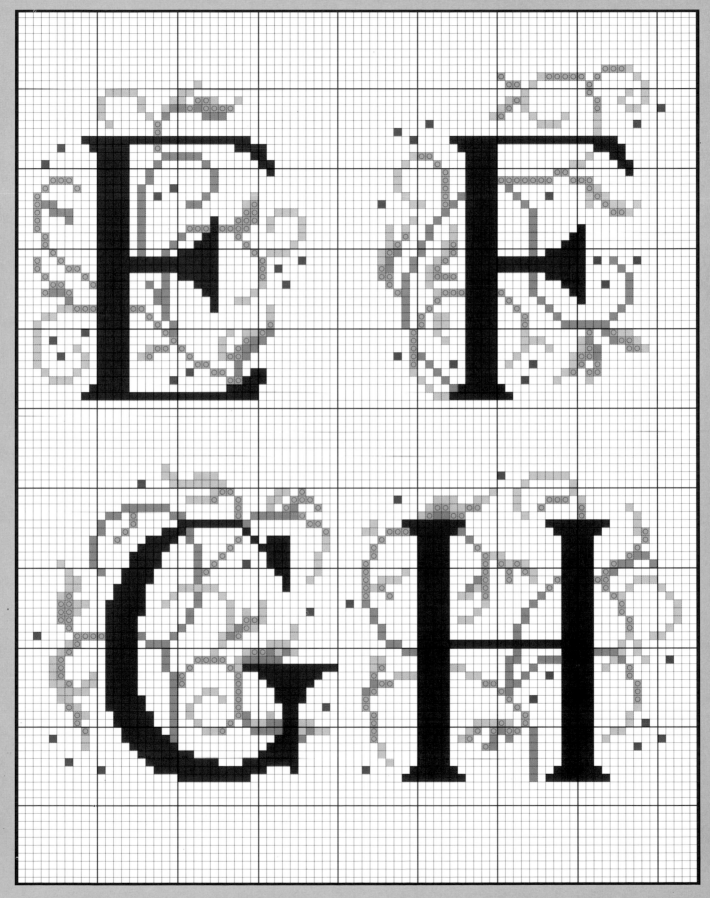

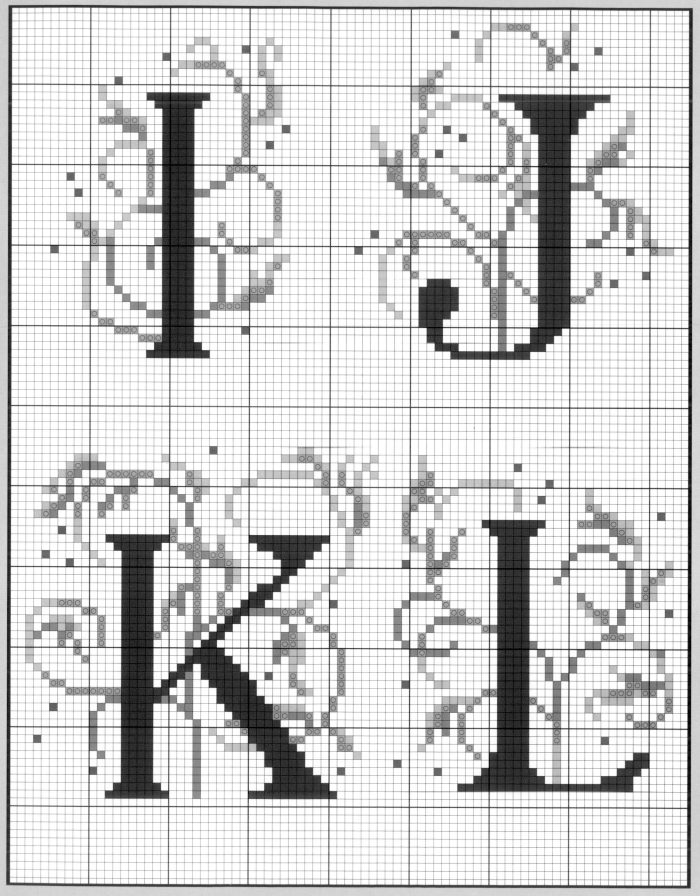

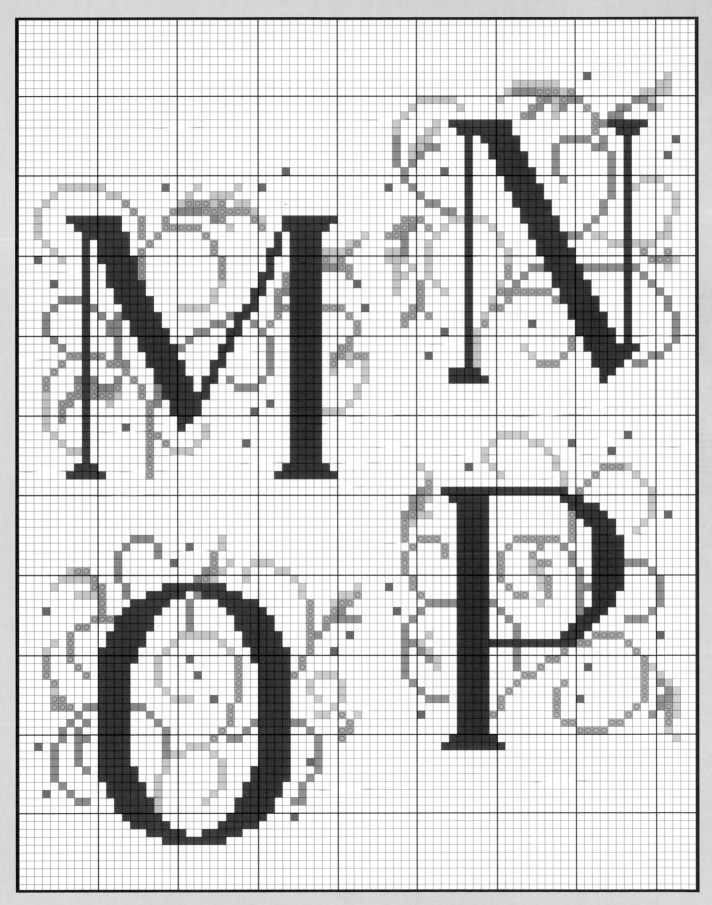

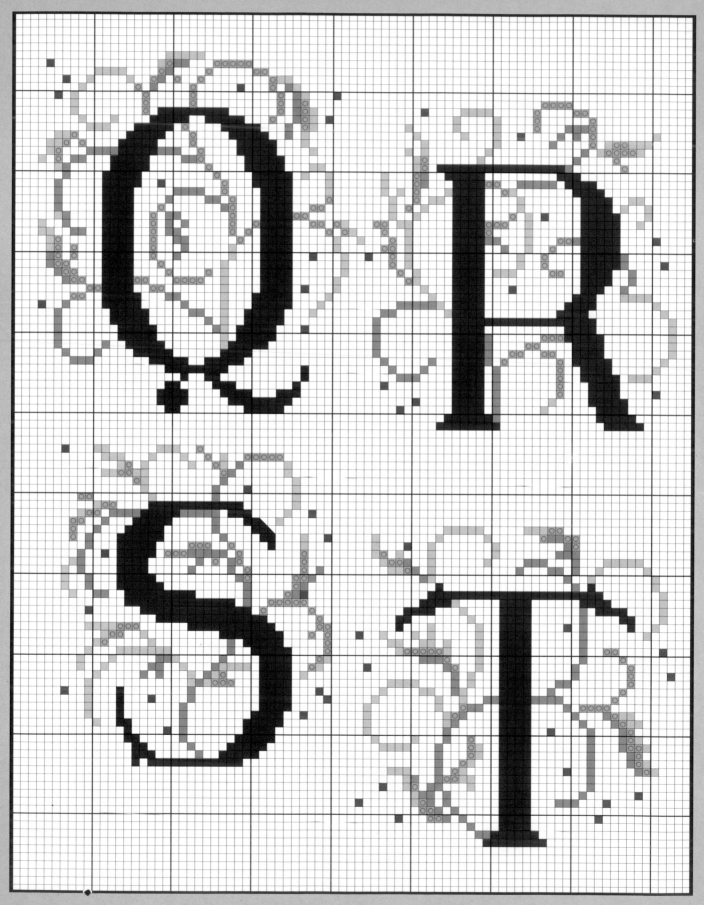

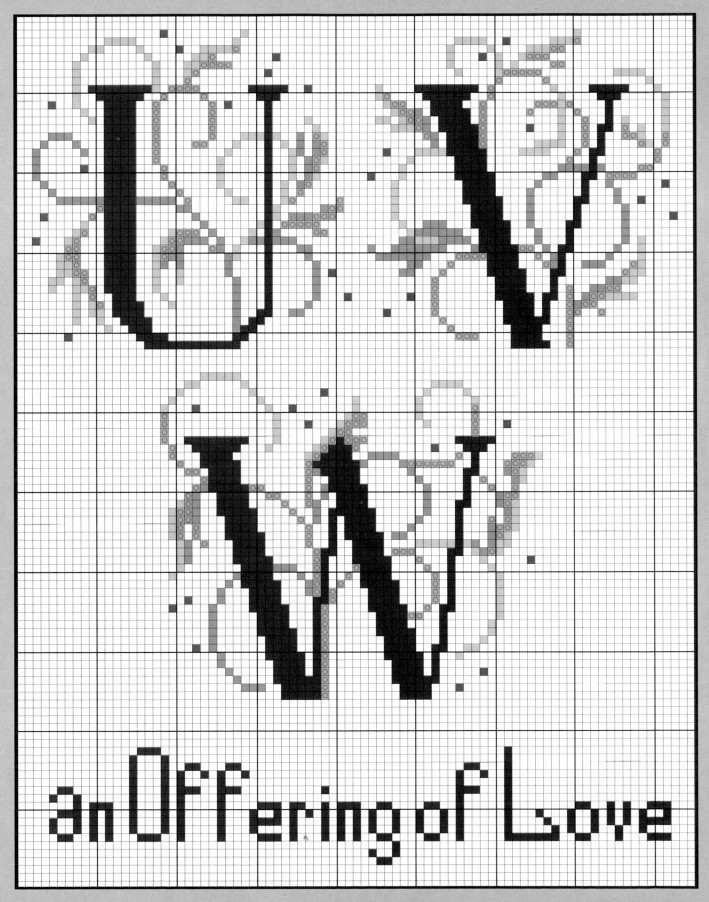

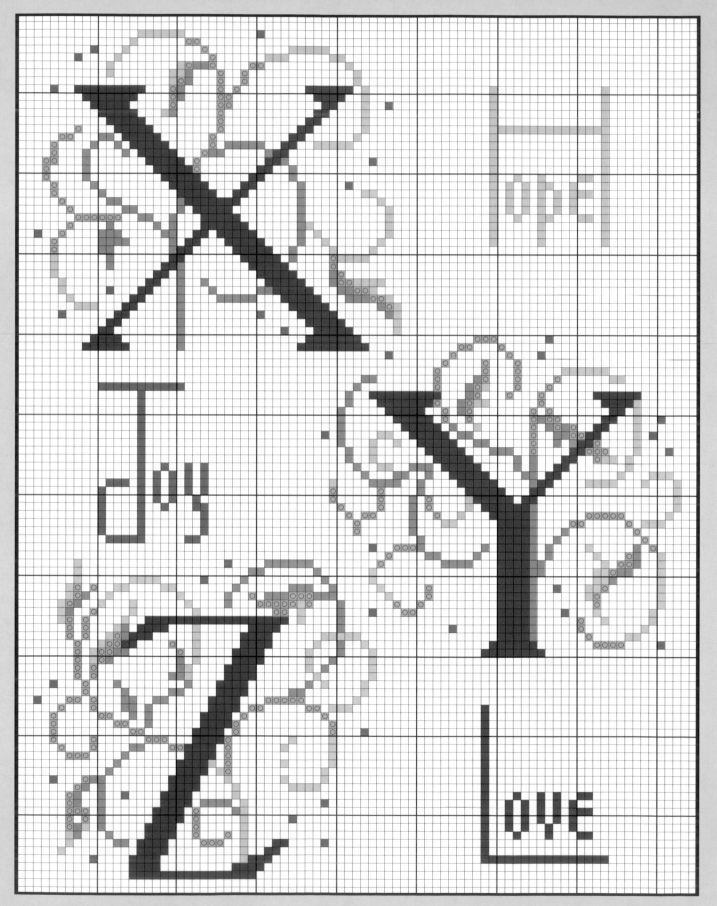

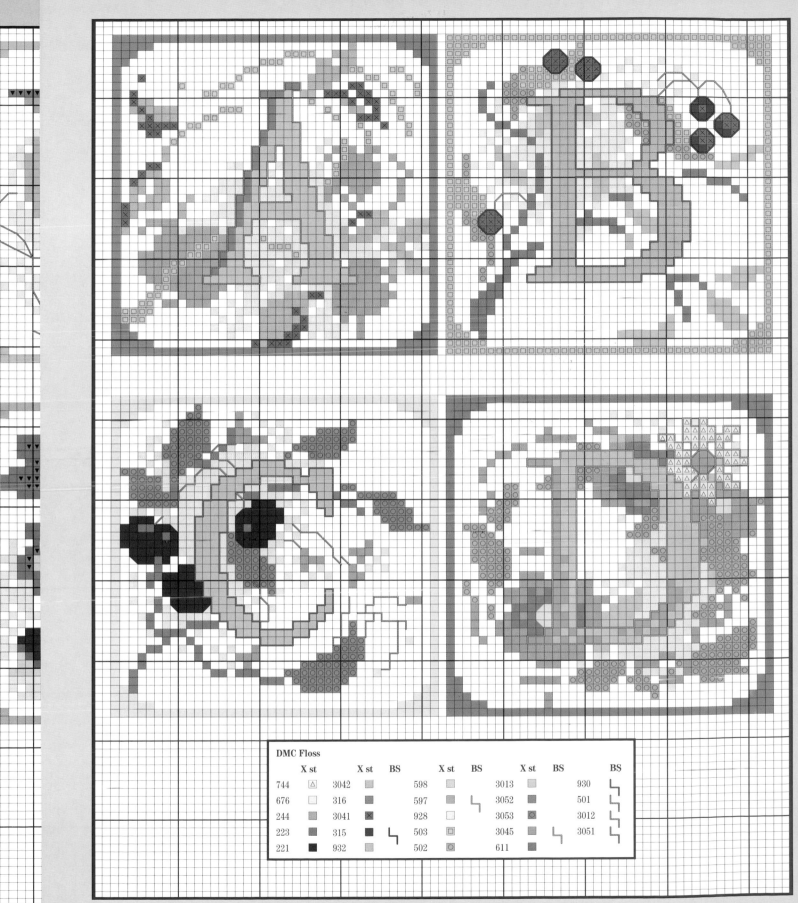

DMC Floss

	X st		X st	BS		X st	BS		X st	BS			BS
744	△	3042	▨		598	▨		3013	▨		930		⌐
676	☐	316	▨		597	▨	⌐	3052	▨		501		⌐
244	▨	3041	▨		928	☐		3053	◉		3012		⌐
223	▨	315	■	⌐	503	▣		3045	▨	⌐	3051		⌐
221	■	932	▨		502	◉		611	▨				

Index